Another
Weird Year 4

Another Weird Year 4

Huw Davies

**cartoons by
Knife and Packer**

EBURY
PRESS

1 3 5 7 9 10 8 6 4 2

Copyright © 2005 Huw Davies

Illustrations © 2005 Knife & Packer

Huw Davies has asserted his moral right to be identified
as the author of this work in accordance with the
Copyright, Designs and Patents Act 1988.

First published 2005 by Ebury Press,
an imprint of Random House,
20 Vauxhall Bridge Road, London SW1V 2SA

Random House Australia (Pty) Limited
20 Alfred Street, Milsons Point, Sydney, New South Wales 2061,
Australia

Random House New Zealand Limited
18 Poland Road, Glenfield, Auckland 10, New Zealand

Random House South Africa (Pty) Limited
Isle of Houghton, Corner of Boundary Road & Carse O'Gowrie,
Houghton 2198, South Africa

The Random House Group Limited Reg. No. 954009

www.randomhouse.co.uk

Printed and bound in Great Britain by Bookmarque Ltd,
Croydon, Surrey

A CIP catalogue record for this book is
available from the British Library

Cover design by Two Associates
Interior design by seagulls

ISBN 0 091908701

Contents

Introduction

Welcome to this fourth collection of the world's weird, wonderful and wacky stories. For those of you new to the concept, *Another Weird Year* is one of the few books that takes the year's weirdness, craziness and stupidity seriously enough to present it all to you in one convenient book. Remember that. You don't need to bother with the newspaper or the TV news or even updates on your PDA – just wait for the next edition of *Another Weird Year* and all you need to know about the world will be revealed to you in one neat package. If you're still unclear on what you'll find inside these pages, let me give you an idea by using some well-known sayings.

'Give a man a fish,' they say, 'and he will eat for a day. But teach him how to fish, and he will eat for a lifetime.' It's a message of hope and faith in the essence of humanity, the value of constructive assistance and thinking long-term for the greater good. Things are *sooo* not like that in the world of *Another Weird Year*. It's more along the lines of 'Teach a man to fish – and he'll sit in a boat drinking beer all day then fall in and drown himself.' Or, as happened in one of the stories you'll find inside here, sit in a boat and blow himself up with dynamite.

'You're unique,' someone might say to you, and add cruelly, 'just like everyone else.' Something else that I always find weird is that when a story emerges that you'd think absolutely has to be unique, at least one more arrives soon after. This happened when I was collecting stories for the first *Another Weird Year*. I found what I thought would be an unrepeatable story about a robber losing an artificial limb but in fact ended up with a little section on crime and artificial limbs. It's happened again: I got a story about a bizarre towing incident, which I foolishly assumed would be the only one to turn up in that year – or any year – and lo and behold a couple of weeks later along came another very similar and equally unnerving story.

'I destroy my enemies when I make them my friends,' Abraham Lincoln is supposed to have said, which was fine for trying to reconcile the warring Northern and Southern states of America, but never seemed to apply to the residents of this book, who bite off their enemies' noses and ears and fingers without a second thought. And mutilate their genitals. That's one way of destroying your enemies, I suppose.

'I love humanity, but I hate people' is another saying. It's the difference between theory and practice. In theory we've all been brought up to be polite and love one another, especially in our own families; but in practice you get a father and son shooting each other over how best to cook chicken for dinner. One marriage in three, they say, ends in divorce, but not all divorces happen after a mere hour and a half of marriage, as you will read here. And if one in three marriages ends in divorce, then doesn't that mean two-thirds of all marriages are happy and harmonious? That would imply that husbands never shut their wives up in the pigsty or chop their tongues off, examples of both of which you will find within these pages.

There's another nice saying: 'Everyone seems normal – until you get to know them.' So come inside and get to know the residents of *Another Weird Year 4* and realise how *sooo* not normal they all are. They'll amuse you, surprise you and occasionally shock you. There's stuff to make you grin, and stuff that is grim – be prepared for anything. And please feel free to wander over to www.anotherweirdyear.com any time you like and send me your own delightful discoveries.

Huw Davies
London, 2005

ANOTHER CRIMINAL YEAR

Yet again we open with Law and Order – because it's the law.

CRIME

A blind man from south-west London received a 16-month prison sentence and had an antisocial behaviour order slapped on him thanks to his rather unusual obsession for groping women while talking about phlegm. Neil Middlehurst's approach to getting a thrill from life was to ask women for help crossing the road, then to feel their breasts while talking about sore throats and the phlegm they produced. Indeed, part of Middlehurst's antisocial behaviour order was a ban on saying the word 'phlegm'.

WEIRD REMOVALS

This is a very weird one – be warned!

 An eight-months-pregnant woman was found strangled to death in the US state of Missouri. Her

getting away with murder

A bizarre story that spans a decade emerged last year after a woman's dramatic deathbed confession. In the US state of Massachusetts, Geraldine Kelley admitted to her children, gathered around her in her last days of life, that their late father hadn't really died in a car crash as they had been told. It seems that she had, in fact, murdered him when they lived in California, concocted the car crash story and placed his body in a freezer, which ended up in a rented storage depot in a Boston suburb when she moved back from California to Massachusetts. After suffering years of domestic abuse Kelley had shot her husband, John, in the head with a handgun. When police went to the depot to check the truth of the story, they discovered a large freezer wrapped up in duct tape and emitting a distinctly corpse-like odour. It wasn't clear at the time of writing how Kelley managed to fake his burial in California, but one thing which *is* clear is that she truly got away with murder.

baby had been cut from her womb and taken away – kidnapped, if you like. Not long afterwards, over the state border in Kansas, a 36-year-old woman was in a café with her husband, proudly showing off their gorgeous new baby to all and sundry before going to visit the church pastor. The husband in question had believed that his wife, Lisa Montgomery, was pregnant; and she had woven a story in which she was pregnant with twins, then had an unusual sort of miscarriage in which just one of the twins died. She then went on a trip to Missouri, from where she phoned her husband to say that she had gone into labour and given birth – when in reality she had murdered Bobbi Jo Stinnett and removed her baby from her womb. Police succeeded in tracking down Montgomery because she had communicated with Stinnett by computer, in a

James Donalson, 59, of the US state of Texas, had been engaged in a long disagreement with the medical company that supplied his mother with a pacemaker for her heart condition. When she died at the age of 85, paramedics came to their home to find that Donalson had taken a kitchen knife, cut open his dead mother's chest and removed the pacemaker. He said that he wanted to keep the pacemaker as evidence of wrongdoing by the company that supplied it, but he was arrested on a charge of tampering with evidence.

chatroom, under an assumed name. The baby, who appeared to be totally unharmed in all of this, was returned to her father.

In the town of Morrisville in the US state of Vermont a 17-year-old boy was arrested for having removed a head from a corpse in a cemetery. Investigating police found a tomb broken into and a head removed from the body of a man; it was believed that the youth planned to use the head as a 'bong' to smoke marijuana through.

Local folk musicians in the Solomon Isles are sabotaging the government's efforts to provide the country with clean drinking water. It seems that as fast as the authorities lay PVC piping to carry clean water to

gasp!

William Armstrong, 56, had to take a very deep breath before he started robbing a store in Akron, Ohio – not because he was nervous, but because of a chronic respiratory condition. However, Armstrong gave up halfway through the raid and asked the shop assistant to pop out to his car and get his oxygen tank for him.

rural communities, pan-pipe musicians dig them up and make them into pan pipes. Pan-pipe bands are popular in the Solomon Isles, and frequently play to tourists, and musicians have stopped using traditional bamboo pipes in favour of PVC. Health authorities have sternly warned that any pan-pipe band found playing on PVC instruments will be questioned.

Work this one out: Mark Shleifer, 48, of the US state of Pennsylvania, pleaded guilty to possessing more than 1000 pictures of child pornography, even though he is legally blind.

Paul Hardy, 40, broke into a couple's home in the US state of West Virginia on New Year's Eve and relieved them of $540 at gunpoint. So far, so basic. But instead of making off with the money, he continued to hold them at gunpoint for over an hour until he noticed that there was a piano, at which point things got a little weird. He commanded the husband to play songs while Hardy sang, and then, clearly in a great mood after a nice singsong, ordered pizzas all round. While they were waiting Hardy toyed idly with his gun, which went off, shooting him by accident and enabling the couple to call the police and end the horror and the weirdness.

WOULD YOU BELIEVE IT

How about these as attempts to explain away a crime?

Sandu Florenta, 18, a Romanian, was arrested for shoplifting at a Tesco in Wrexham. In a special bag that she had concealed under her clothing she had managed to secrete: 'four packs of frozen lamb, three fresh chickens, three packs of stock cubes, finger chillies, a packet of burgers, garlic, peppers, socks and underwear, plus almost five pounds of oranges and apples', according to Tesco. Florenta told

Showing a highly developed sense of irony, an escaped convict in Germany was arrested when he was discovered posing as a police officer in the town of Bernau. Not just any old policeman, though. He had stolen a car, equipped it with a blue roof light and had been adding to his meagre income by carrying out routine traffic controls and taking on-the-spot fines from drivers. The man was wanted by police in Hanover, where he had absconded from home leave, and faced an additional sentence for his new crime.

the arresting officers that this was the normal way to shop in Romania, where not many stores have shopping trolleys.

Possibly the worst excuse heard in a court of law last year? Farmhand Dean Schwankert, 37, of the US state of New Hampshire, was up in court on a charge of lewdness. He had allegedly stripped naked and chased his employer – a 75-year-old woman – around her house, asking for sex. Schwankert told police he was merely making a nude enquiry as to what time it was.

LOOK INTO MY EYES, JUST THE EYES ...

Assisted robberies, and other scams ...

In Italy, a criminal masquerading as a priest was caught on CCTV stealing from shopkeepers in a very unusual way. Film footage showed the man going into a jeweller's and hypnotising the shopkeeper, who then opened the till and handed over wads of cash.

In Cape Town, South Africa, two men and a woman wheeled old Thozamile Apolis into a bank to 'help' him withdraw his pension. Only problem was that Apolis was dead, and this fact was not lost on the bank clerk, especially when they tried to make Apolis's hand 'sign' for the pension by moving it across the paper. When asked to prove that their friend had a pulse, the three masterminds fled, leaving the corpse behind.

 A restaurant in Soderhamn, Sweden, received a visit from a man who said he was the local council's alcohol inspector. His job was to check the alcohol content of every type of drink served in the restaurant, he said, so a glass of each was lined up for him to sample. He got stuck into the testing with such gusto that he shortly became quite drunk and started throwing things around, at which point it dawned on the owners that they were dealing with an imposter. They swiftly called the police.

Meanwhile the driver with the freshest breath would have been Carol Ries from Michigan, USA, who was pulled over by police after a minor crash, and then failed an alcohol test. Ries admitted to having drunk three glasses of Listerine earlier, and as a result was three times over the legal blood-alcohol limit. Original-formula Listerine has about 26 per cent alcohol, making it twice as strong as wine. And with a fresher taste.

Compare and contrast the Listerine-drunk driver with this one: in Ontario, Canada, traffic cops

BIZARRE

Sometimes hotel guests steal the towels or help themselves to a teaspoon or two – but the couple who spent the night at the seventeenth-century Globe Hotel in Topsham, Exeter, managed to get away with the shower. The hotel management said that the whole shower unit had been dismantled and removed, and since the couple had paid for their room in cash it would be very hard to trace them.

pulled over a drink driver. They hauled him into the back of their police car and took him to the station to have a breathalyser test. The 59-year-old man had a bit of an accident on the way there, throwing up, and emptying his bowels in the back of the car. As they pulled into the station, he grabbed a handful of his own faeces and stuffed it into his mouth so that the breathalyser machine would malfunction. It didn't. The shitfaced, shitty-arsed motorist was successfully charged with drunk driving. And his wife wouldn't kiss him when he got home.

Romanian police in the southern town of Pitesti stopped Ruxandra Gardian and her friend when an eyewitness alerted them to the fact that the two women appeared to have stolen a mobile phone from a customer in a shop. The officers searched the women but no phone was found. As a last resort the phone's owner called the number of his phone – and a ringtone was heard drifting from between Gardian's legs. A more intimate search at the police station revealed that she had indeed stolen the phone and swiftly secreted it up her front bottom. The owner refused to take it back, too, so there were no winners.

UNUSUAL

A man was arrested in Brazil for what a police spokesman called 'the weirdest robbery I have ever heard of'. The 18-year-old threatened a priest, Francisco Eloi de Souza, with that scariest of weapons – a butter knife – and stole two Bibles which the priest had just bought, before running away through the streets of Boa Viagem. The priest alerted a nearby policeman who quickly caught up with the robber and arrested him.

Another Weird Year has reported police discovering all sorts of unusual illicit operations, but maybe none on the scale of this story. Italian police came upon an entire racecourse, complete with grandstands, a car park and 80 racehorses, all in a secret location near Naples. The course was built without planning permission, so never appeared on any official documents, and when it was raided by paramilitary *carabinieri*, over 200 cars were parked there, while the stables were found to have thousands of packets of drugs for doping the horses, including Viagra, which as well as turning men into stallions also makes horses go faster.

STUPID CRIMS

Careful planning, rational, logical thought, an intelligent approach – these crims display none of these ...

A would-be bank robber burst into a bank in the US state of Florida and shouted, 'Freeze, mother-stickers, this is a fuck-up.' Everyone in the bank burst out laughing and the man turned and ran in total and utter humiliation.

A Cambodian man attempted to claim on his life insurance policy by faking his own death. So he bought a corpse for $1500 (no, we don't know where one buys corpses in Cambodia), placed it carefully in the driver's seat of his own car, rolled the car down a hill, torched it and then made his claim. All perfectly in order as far as faking your own death goes, except for one crucial thing that came to light in the investigation: the corpse he had bought was of a young woman.

Faking your own death and ultimately failing is also the theme of this story from the US state of Texas, where Molly Daniels pleaded guilty to helping her husband Clayton fake his own death in order to collect on the insurance. The couple dug up a body from a cemetery, put it in the driver's seat of his car and set the car on fire to make it look as though he had been in a fatal accident. They even went as far as introducing Molly Daniels's four-year-old son to her 'new boyfriend' – actually Clayton Daniels with his hair dyed black. Investigators into the car accident found that the corpse was that of an 81-year-old

Irishman Brendan Mahoney tried to cash an unemployment benefit cheque in a Birmingham post office, but the idiot had little hope of getting the money: Mr Mahoney's very strong Irish accent and non-Asian appearance contrasted fairly clearly with the name on the cheque of Abdul Khaliq. A birth certificate with 'Mahoney' crossed out and 'Khaliq' written in was not very convincing either.

woman rather than a middle-aged man, and although the car was found at the bottom of a cliff there were no skid marks on the road. And the car fire had clearly been started by a cigarette lighter left on the front seat. That all adds up to a very fine example of criminal stupidity.

No points for intelligence for the robber who hit a drive-through chicken restaurant in the US state of Louisiana. He told all the employees in the restaurant to run for it, which to a man they did – leaving no one to open the till or the safe.

Desperately dumb déjà vu: a Romanian man was jailed four years ago for burgling the flat of a wealthy neighbour. Just hours after being released from jail, and presumably thinking only that the neighbour would have had plenty of time to restock his valuables, Ionel Raileanu went straight back to the same flat and broke in. Neighbours raised the alarm, an officer from the local police station – the very same officer who had arrested him the first time – whizzed down, and Raileanu was caught coming out of the flat with money, jewellery and a computer. And it was straight back to the same jail, only this time for a 15-year stretch.

Albania's most wanted criminal dodged the police for years, but last year blew himself up on a dynamite fishing trip. Riza Malaj had been sentenced in his absence to five years in prison for leading an attack on

STUPID

A 42-year-old man was astonished when he was arrested for a bank robbery just minutes afterwards, even though he thought he was in the perfect disguise. Merle Hatch robbed a bank in Denver in the US state of Colorado, quickly changed into running shorts and trainers and went on his way as an apparently innocent jogger. But – and this is the monumentally stupid bit – he got changed in full view of the bank staff, who simply told police when they arrived exactly what he was wearing.

a police station, and was the subject of warrants for arrest for murder, armed assault and battery, and was nicknamed 'The Last Cowboy' because of his frequent gun battles with police. But he ended up in hospital in terrible shape after misjudging the length of fuse on a stick of dynamite he was using to blow up trout. Malaj lost both hands and suffered injuries to his eyes and the rest of his body, but since his family took him to hospital across the border in Kosovo, his capture by Albanian police may have to wait a while yet.

Thanh Nhat Le, 51, was arrested in the US state of Massachusetts after being almost delightfully dumb. Le had opened a bank account at a Sovereign Bank, with the princely sum of $171, all in small denomination notes. Then, after, depositing a couple of cheques into the account, he tried to write himself a cheque for cash, to the amount of $7550. Now, what could have given his attempted deceit away? His laughably naive scam was to post three cheques to be paid into his account: one for $250,000, one for $2 million, and one for $4 billion.

SPUNKY CRIMS

Last year we had a young men tricking women into rubbing his semen into their faces. This year a nightshift cook at a fast-food restaurant in the US state of Illinois was found to have added the same special ingredient to food he was preparing, then watching as the unsuspecting customers ate it. Anthony Lindhorst, 26, put his own semen into the honey mustard dressing served with chicken strips, targeting people he didn't like – a police officer who had issued a traffic ticket to Lindhorst, for example – then looking on while they enjoyed their added-protein meal. Witnesses to the incidents – possibly disgusted co-workers – grassed him up to the police.

An American dentist had his licence revoked by the North Carolina Board of Dental Examiners when it was found that he had been injecting his semen into the mouths of several patients. First he tearfully denied the charges, but when his semen was found on syringes handed in by two of his assistants, and patients testified to an 'awful'-tasting substance he had squirted into their mouths, he said that the reason he had his own semen in the office was for a sperm-count test concerning his use of a hair-loss drug.

GIVING THEM MORE THAN THEY BARGAINED FOR

The weirder ways of fighting back against crime and foiling criminals ...

In San Francisco, burglar Juan Garcia Vasquez broke into the apartment of a 73-year-old woman one night. She was woken by the sound of breaking glass, went to see what was happening and came face to face with the intruder. She lulled him into a false sense of security by offering him food, which he accepted, and while he was eating she launched her secret weapon – family photos. She sat next to him on the couch and showed him snaps of her grandchildren.

Eighty-eight-year-old Gerhard Brinkmann was visiting a friend's grave in the north German town of Halberstadt when he was accosted by a nasty young man who demanded his wallet and watch. The apparently frail old Mr Brinkmann had been the German lightweight boxing champion in 1936, and despite his age still knew how to deliver a decent punch. As the would-be mugger came within range Brinkmann landed a perfect right hook to his chin and down he went – a knockout! While Brinkmann called the police, the mugger regained consciousness and made a break for it, and as Brinkmann said, although he could still punch, at 88 he couldn't run too well.

Poor Vasquez was powerless to resist, and before long he dozed off, enabling her to call the police.

A grandmother in Cornwall was woken at 5 am one morning by a noise and rushed out of her house in her nightdress to find a burglar clambering on her roof. Jean Collop, 69, snatched up a garden gnome, took aim, and launched it at the man. The gnome cannoned into the man's head and knocked him out. Jean then ran back inside for weapon number two, her rolling pin, and a camera. When she came out the burglar was still unconscious, so she took some photos of him for good measure, while neighbours called the police. When they arrived, the man was still on the roof, dazed, and a group of neighbours were standing guard below, with Jean still holding her rolling pin. She said later that she

divine retribution

In the Romanian city of Sibiu a pick-pocket dipped his hand into the pocket of a man waiting at a bus stop and stole some money from him. His victim twigged what was going on and immediately gave chase, pursuing the robber through the streets. The chase didn't last long, as the robber collapsed and died of a heart attack.

got it because she didn't want to break another gnome on the burglar. He was probably very relieved to be taken away by the police.

PRISON LIFE

Just to remind them that they were his bitches, so to speak, Sheriff Joe Arpaio (America's toughest sheriff, apparently) made 700 hardened prisoners walk the two miles from their old maximum security jail to a new one, wearing nothing but shocking pink under-wear and flip-flops. Oh and their tattoos. The inmates had all been due to be transferred from their old, over-crowded jail to a new jail, and Sheriff Arpaio decided that chaining them all together by the ankle and making them wear women's clothing would send out a message to everyone who witnessed the humiliating parade. (And that would be, if you're a tough man who likes to wear women's underwear, get sent to Sheriff Arpaio's prison.)

A search of prisoners in Australia's Grafton Prison revealed that some inmates were in possession of the venomous redback spider. The spiders were not used for threatening other prisoners, but for milking. The venom was milked by inmates to produce a toxin they injected to get high.

In Perth, Scotland, convicted drug dealer Colin Hancock saw the doctor when suffering from symptoms of urine blockage, but was extremely disconcerted when he was examined. Dr Alexander MacFarlane needed to carry out a rectal examination, but the only substance available as a lubricant was milk from a bowl of porridge. Hancock sued.

In a Norwegian prison, a Vietnamese man, convicted of the double murder of a woman and her son, used a hydraulic cutting device in a workshop to cut off both his own legs and one hand – then sued prison authorities for not having watched over him closely enough.

What are things coming to when prisoners are treated like nothing more than criminals? A full-page ad appeared in a Mexican daily newspaper, *Reforma*, after the country's president, Vicente Fox, cracked down on prison corruption. The ad was placed by some of the inmates in La Palma jail, near Mexico City, and complained that they were now 'suffering under sub-human conditions, treated like dogs, like animals, like we are worthless, like the scum of society'. What terrible ills had the poor prisoners (mostly drug barons and leaders of organised crime rackets) in question suffered to make them feel like scum? Their wide-screen TVs had been confiscated; their computers had

A 35-year-old Serb prisoner in an Austrian jail, who was serving a three-month sentence for a traffic offence, got himself into deeper doo-doo when he blabbed about another crime he had committed. The man, named as Roberto, told his cellmate how he had conned an Austrian woman out of £5000 for a non-existent business venture and also got her to sign up for some company mobile phones, with which he ran up bills of around £2500, all without being caught. As luck would have it, the cellmate to whom he was boasting was the woman's husband. He wasted no time in reporting Roberto, who was sentenced to a further 18 months in prison and told to repay the woman the money by the county court in Vienna.

QUIRKY

been confiscated; and their mobile phones, which they were using to carry on their criminal operations, were confiscated. Oh, and their personal pizza deliveries had been stopped. Life's tough, guys.

Possibly in an effort to help their victims see the funny side of being mugged, burgled and so on, prisoners at Winchester jail were allowed to go on comedy courses last year. The scheme, funded jointly by a comedy bar chain and public money, has comedians teaching 400 inmates how to do stand-up comedy. A prison spokesman said that the course teaches inmates, 'Communication powers of empathy and humility'.

And from Japan, a move to make life less stressful for criminals came to our attention last year. The idea was to try to improve morale among the prison population by giving prisoners attractively coloured uniforms and bedding. Government advisers were of the opinion that there was a tasteless clash of colours between the stripes of orange and green on prison bedsheets, and that this would make prisoners nervous and aggressive, while their black-and-white-striped pyjamas and green uniforms were slated as lacking brightness. The psychologists' recommendations were for brown bedding and for their day outfits to be in a fetching mint green and pale blue. That way, the prisoners get a more positive outlook – and better fashion sense when they get out.

GETTING OUT OF JAIL

A Czech prisoner banged up for a six-month stretch for theft was set free because he woke up one morning with an erection that just would not go away. The 37-year-old told prison officers that he was in a great deal of pain, and prison doctors who took a look at his unwiltingly solid manhood were unable to help. The prisoner was taken to a specialist hospital for surgery, and then allowed home to be looked after by his – probably very excited – wife.

It's not how the turban is intended to be used, so full marks for creativity go to the seven prisoners, including some convicted of murder, who escaped from a Pakistani jail by unravelling their turbans and using them as ropes. The prisoners broke through a toilet window in the jail in Machh, 50 km south of the city of Quetta, then scaled the high-security jail's perimeter wall with the turbans.

Joseph Holland, 23, escaped from prison in the US state of Pennsylvania, was captured the very next day, and had a charge against his name for escaping. Holland contacted a judge directly to dispute the charge on the following counts: (a) he had not been told he wasn't allowed to escape; (b) since he was gone for just 24 hours and all his belongings were still in the prison, how can anyone prove that he didn't intend to come straight back? And (c) the guards opened the gate to let him out (in fact they opened the gate to let a prisoner in, and Holland sneaked out unnoticed). We think (a) and (b) at least are very good points indeed.

THE LAW

Thirty-five years passed between a man being stabbed and his eventual death – and a court ruled that he had been murdered. George Stockley suffered a stomach wound when he was stabbed in 1969 in New York City. In 2004 he had surgery to remove some of the scar tissue from the wound, got an infection and died. His death was classified as murder by the authorities on the grounds that it came as a result of the original stabbing. There was no murder investigation because the man who was the chief suspect in the crime died in 1997.

Flattery will get you nowhere, they say; but in Costa Rica now it may get you somewhere – prison. A new law was passed in Costa Rica last year that might just make life a little difficult for men – in effect, a man can now get sent to jail for trying to chat up a woman. The new law allows women to have a man arrested for paying them unwanted compliments. Offenders will be faced with punishments of a fine or up to 50 days in prison. A police spokesmen said that although it might be difficult to enforce this new law, they would trust women's judgement.

Holland is renowned for its liberalism, so it may come as no surprise to hear that a Dutch court allowed a bank robber to claim the cost of a pistol used in a hold-up as a legitimate business expense. The judge at Breda Criminal Court permitted the 46-year-old man to set the cost of the gun – 2000 guilders – against his gross proceeds of 6750 guilders, gained during his raid on a bank in the southern town of Chaam. The judge duly reduced the robber's fine by the same amount, then sentenced him to four years in jail. A spokesman for the Dutch prosecutors' service said the judge had followed sound legal precedents on the confiscation of criminal assets. Leendert De Lange said: 'The idea is that crime does not pay, but you are allowed to claim your expenses.'

The government of North Korea is not passing a law, as far as we know, about hair length, but it is actively encouraging, even ordering, its male citizens to sort themselves out. The (state-run) television station in the nation's capital, Pyongyang, launched an ad campaign with the snappy title of 'Let Us Trim Our Hair In Accordance With Socialist Lifestyle'. The message to North Korea's menfolk is to get their hair trimmed every 15 days, and the campaign even named and shamed individuals whose locks were overly flowing. Long hair, according to the programme, uses energy that ought to be reserved for the brain, hence a nice neat trim also means sharper thinking. Oh, if only it were true. Men over 50, it seems, are allowed an extra 7 cm for an image-protecting comb-over.

Immigrants to Canada who are seeking work as strippers – and there are a fair few, apparently – are now required by law to submit nude performance photos of themselves. It would seem that too many people have been slipping into Canada falsely claiming to be strippers, so candidates have to prove that they look acceptable naked – and the photos have to show them fully nude, otherwise no go. I wonder who gets the job of vetting these immigrants?

How much of a weird ass can the law be? In Texas, Jimmy Dean Watkins pleaded guilty to shooting his estranged wife to death, and also to wounding her boyfriend. For the killing of his wife, Watkins was sentenced to a mere four months in prison – and 15 years for the wounding. The jury found that he had killed his wife with partially excusable 'sudden passion' when he found her with the boyfriend, but that shooting the boyfriend was more deliberate.

THE PETTY ARM OF THE LAW

As police officers were busy setting up a radar trap in the town of Jessen, in eastern Germany, they fell foul of the petty inclinations of a traffic policeman who saw they had parked their squad car on the wrong side of the road. Seconds later, he issued them with a parking

Poor old Sergio Segundo Ruiz, 60, was hit by a car when crossing a street in his home city of Ciudad Juarez, Mexico, and was hospitalised with multiple injuries. Nevertheless, Ruiz was charged with interfering with traffic, and a police officer was stationed outside his room to arrest him as soon as he was recovered enough from his injuries to leave.

INSANE

ticket. 'Traffic regulations apply to everyone,' a town hall spokesperson primly remarked later.

The petty arm of the law caught up with an Argentinian rock star last year after a long chase – ten years in fact. 'I feel so good that I could smoke a joint,' Andres Calamaro told a crowd of 100,000 fans on 19 November 1994 in La Plata, south of Buenos Aires. Angry parents tried to prosecute Calamaro, now 43, and a judge dismissed the charges; but a decade later, those parents finally found a more hard-line judge and Calamaro again faced criminal proceedings for his dreadful admission.

A motorist suffered at the hands of pettiness after he stopped to give first-aid to a road accident victim in Wood Green, London. Jake Fury, a qualified first-aider, ran to help a 13-year-old girl who had been hit by a car. As the girl lay there screaming in pain, Mr Fury competently attended to her, called an ambulance and comforted her. Then he noticed that a parking attendant was giving him a ticket for stopping his car in an unauthorised area, and later received a £100 fine.

LAWSUITS AND COURT CASES

Pole drives Pole up the pole. Piotr Kardys, a businessman from the Polish city of Kolbuszowa, was in dispute with Polish telephone company TPSA about the small matter of a telephone pole in his kitchen. TPSA put up the pole on land owned by Kardys without his permission, and when he built his house on his property he had no choice but to build round the pole, which ended up in the middle of his kitchen. Local authorities rescinded the building permit for the pole and told TPSA to move it, but TPSA spokeswoman Izabella Szum said the company would appeal.

A self-employed German man received a tax bill in error, for a massive £200 million. Since he only earned around £12,000 a year, he knew that he could successfully challenge the tax demand in court, and hired a lawyer to sort things out for him. So far, so good – except he didn't reckon on the fact that German lawyers are entitled to a percentage of the amount of money they save for their clients. Remember, the demand was for £200 million, so his lawyer eventually presented him with a bill for £1.5 million.

As a pleasant surprise for some of their neighbours, two sweet teenage girls in the US state of Colorado baked cookies and left them on their doorsteps, along with cut-out paper hearts and a message that read, 'Have a great night.' A lovely gesture, I'm sure you'll agree. And there's more – the girls had the choice that night of going out to a dance or staying home and baking the cookies, and they self-lessly chose the latter. So it may come as a surprise to hear that one of those neighbours sued the two girls on the grounds that the delivery of unsolicited cookies onto her doorstep at the ungodly hour of 10.30 pm caused her so much distress that an anxiety attack was triggered and she had to go to hospital the next day. And the judge who heard the case ordered the girls to pay $900 in medical costs and court costs, agreeing that 10.30 was a little late to be out and this made their action rather scary.

Antoinette Millard, 40, of New York, filed a lawsuit against credit card company American Express demanding that they cancel her credit card charges. Millard said that far from her debt being her own respon-sibility, American Express were totally and utterly to blame for her $950,000 – that's nearly a million dollars, folks – shopping spree at the swankiest shops in New York City. After all, they had been stupid enough to issue her with the top-range, in credit terms, Centurion card. And anyway, the lawsuit stated, Millard suffers from anorexia, depression, panic attacks and head tumours which combine to make her a desperately out-of-control

Old joke: (Patient) 'Doctor, doctor, I've only got 59 seconds to live.' (Doctor) 'Hang on a minute.' *Real life story*: a man given six months to live by his doctors was told by an Italian court to come back to hear the outcome of his demand for insurance damages – in 14 months. Carmelo Cisabella, 39, suffering from an inoperable spine disease, was keen to recover €450,000 in agreed damages from his insurers to help ease the final few months of life. Cisabella tried to get the Sicilian courts to hurry up the slow-moving insurers, but was told to return next year to hear their decision.

impulse shopper, unable to curb her spending urges. She just might not win that one.

A trial at Swansea crown court had to be stopped when it was discovered that one of the jurors had not heard most of the evidence because his ears were blocked. The trial was of a man charged with threats to kill, and the juror sat through the whole of the first day quite happily before another juror mentioned the problem to a court official at the start of the second day. When questioned, the juror admitted he had not heard most of the evidence because his ears were blocked after a heavy cold. Judge Christopher Morton was obliged to discharge the jury and order a new trial.

How can you be in the wrong and still win your case? Australian Philip Dederer, 20, trespassed on private property and ignored 'No Diving' signs to jump repeatedly in the Wallamba River. Dederer seriously injured himself in so doing, ending up a paraplegic, but was awarded around £500,000 by a sympathetic judge who thought that the signs were not an adequate warning of the dangers of diving.

In a similar case, Carl Murphy, 18, received £567,000 because when he was trying to rob a warehouse in his home town of Liverpool he fell from the roof. Murphy has several metal plates in his head and has damaged eyesight as a result of the 40-foot fall, and eventually sued the company that owned the warehouse on the grounds that if the perimeter fence had not been broken he could not have got in and gained access to the warehouse. Murphy told reporters that he was going to buy a flash car and a house for his mother to live in when she gets out of jail.

RUBBISH COPS

We're not saying that all police officers have to be as hard as nails, but some element of toughness would seem be a prerequisite for the job. So the Indian policeman who caught a burglar red-handed but then fainted because he thought it was a ghost lacks, we think, the necessary steel to be a good officer. Sub-inspector Ramkailash Dangi, of the state of Madhya Pradesh, heard a noise coming from the locked home of a colleague who had recently been killed in a shoot-out. He went to investigate, saw a figure in the house and fainted dead away, thinking it was the ghost of his late colleague. The next morning, a security guard surveyed a very sorry scene: Dangi was still lying outside the door and bags of valuables that the burglar left behind when he was disturbed were still inside the looted house.

Police in the US state of Ohio decided to reopen an investigation – those geniuses of deduction eventually concluded that a body that had been found shot, wrapped in a blanket, burned and sealed under floorboards was not a suicide.

Two San Francisco police officers were found to have been supplementing their income by starring in a hardcore porn movie. The officers, one man and one woman, played the lead roles in a 45-minute film called *Bus Stop Whores*. The man was removed from the beat and put into a desk job, but his co-star, who works for the Sheriff's Department, stayed in her post at San Francisco General Hospital. Her bosses suspected that this was not a one-off, and that she had made more films, attended adult film conventions and even run her own adult website under the name Reina Leone. As long as they haven't broken the law they keep their jobs – whether they have been setting a good example or not is apparently not too relevant in good ol' San Francisco.

Last year this driving debacle was committed by an elderly man who may not have had all his marbles rattling around his head. This time, a lovelorn Italian policeman was at it: a 23-year-old officer was arrested after driving almost 20 miles the wrong way down a busy motorway and said when he was apprehended that he thought everyone else was driving in the wrong direction. Traffic police, informed of the drunken driver by motorists, only managed to stop him by blocking the stretch of motorway, between Florence and Rome, with sandbags. He told officers that he had begun drinking because of problems with his love life.

A Swedish police officer robbed a bank in the town of Bollnas and then investigated the crime himself just one hour later; he told reporters at the scene of the

cops with integrity

It's all too easy to regard police officers as always ready to take a backhander to ignore crime. But here's a story that proves that there are still some officers who are honourable. A Florida policeman was offered a bribe he could so, so easily have accepted in order to overlook an offence, but he was having none of it. Officer Mark Eastly arrested Steven Denton in the Florida town of Marathon after a fight at a pub. Denton then told Eastly that if he drove him to McDonald's, he would buy him two (two!) cheeseburgers as long as Eastly let him go free. But the incorruptible Officer Eastly not only refused, but added a bribery charge to the assault charge.

crime that the police had no clues. The 36-year-old cop then fell under suspicion when he bought a brand-new Saab, worth around £17,500, for cash not long after the crime, and the cash turned out to be from the robbery.

A Romanian traffic policeman got his come-uppance after he fined a driver for something that had nothing to do with his driving conduct. Marius Vlasceanu stopped Gheorghe Tosa as he drove through the town of Craiova, fined him £22 and handed him a ticket explaining the reason for the fine was 'having a face like a moron and being a big monkey'. Head of the Romanian police Dan Fatuloiu said Vlasceanu had been taken off that job and given a desk job in a remote village.

THE PARANOID ARM OF THE LAW

Blair Davis, a landscape gardener who lives in Houston, Texas, was subject to a shock raid from the Narcotics Task Force. They swooped on his pleasant suburban garden and interrogated him after a neighbour had reported Davis for growing marijuana. The gardener was growing nothing more than the Texas Star hibiscus, a plant that sometimes bears a slight resemblance to marijuana, but the Task Force members, who ought to be expert in these matters, didn't spot this, and not only carried out questioning, but asked Davis suspiciously

The Design Review Board in the town of Snohomish, in the US state of Washington, rejected plans for a mural to be painted on the side of the BBQ Shack restaurant. The owner said it was because its five pink pigs were naked.

WEIRD

what was the purpose of the watermelons and cantaloupes also growing in his garden.

A special needs teacher in the USA was charged at an airport with carrying a concealed weapon. Well, security certainly needs to be toughened up these days, but what exactly did the paranoid law-enforcers identify as her weapon of terror? A bookmark. Kathryn Harrington, 52, suffered the humiliation of being hand-cuffed and taken to a police car to be charged, after screeners saw her leather bookmark with two tiny lead weights at each end. The weights were to stop it slipping out of the book, obviously, but these were seen as a weapon that 'could knock people unconscious'. Not surprisingly, there was no prosecution.

Pillars of the Community

Where would we be without these beacons of exemplary behaviour to guide us?

PRIESTS

Nachum Shifren, 53, is an ultra-Orthodox rabbi, so the long beard and the *kipah* (skullcap) are obligatory. But with the long beard comes a longboard, because Shifren is 'Shifty', a regular figure on the beach at Malibu, southern California, where he is a legendary surf dude rabbi. Shifren says he is ready to surf 24/6, to allow for the Sabbath, and he leads 'Passover surfaris' and beach bar mitzvahs. 'The world of surfing,' says Shifty, 'reflects the hand of the Creator.'

New York City health officials were investigating the death of a baby shortly after a circumcision by Rabbi Yitzchok Fischer. Rabbi Fischer uses a rare, ultra-Orthodox procedure of drawing the infant's blood with his mouth, and officials found that the baby and two others circumcised by Rabbi Fischer had contracted herpes.

POLITICIANS

Canada's immigration minister, Judy Sgro, was forced to resign after pizza restaurant owner Harjit Singh accused her of backing out of a deal she was alleged to have struck with him. Sgro proposed that she would help Singh with an immigration problem if he would deliver pizza and garlic bread to her campaign headquarters.

Senior Cambodian minister Lim El Djurado, in the Ministry of Social Affairs in Phnom Penh, told reporters that he saw no need to resign over the fact that he was supplementing his income in an unorthodox way. Government moves to confiscate pornographic magazines from Cambodian news-stands had led to the revelation that El Djurado was the publisher of two porn magazines, *Teenage Stimulation* and *Rooster*. He pointed out that it was true that he was the publisher of two of Cambodia's leading pornographic magazines, as well as their chief writer, but that he only wrote them at weekends. He added that his ministerial salary was not enough to live on, so without his porn moonlighting he could not continue his worthy work as a government minister. Much of his porn income went towards his daughters' university fees; and they repaid his investment in their education by helping design and lay out the pages.

JUDGES

In the last edition of *Another Weird Year* we had a judge playing with himself in court – now this: a judge in the American state of Oklahoma was seen using a penis pump while trying cases in court. Witnesses said they heard a 'whooshing' noise as Judge Donald Thompson, 57, fumbled inside his robes; a police officer stated that he saw him pumping a tube between his legs and Court Clerk Lisa Foster said that his antics meant that she caught sight of his penis at least 20 times. Judge Thompson said the device was a joke gift from a friend. So that makes it OK, does it?

Faith Johnson, a judge in the US city of Dallas, showed a rather black sense of humour when a convict returned to her court. Billy Williams escaped during his trial for serious assault, was found guilty in his absence and after a year on the run was recaptured and brought back to court to receive his sentence. Judge Johnson made sure it was a sentencing he'd never forget, as Williams was greeted with party hats, streamers, balloons and a 'Welcome' cake – then sentenced to life imprisonment.

LAWYERS

In the US state of Florida, a not-very-sober professional by the name of Albert Tasker, a prosecutor for the County Attorney's Office, thought it would be hilarious to sprint naked across a car park before leaping into the safety of a pal's car. Off came the clothes, off he sprinted across the car park and into his friend's car he leapt. Except Tasker got into a car occupied by a woman waiting for her boyfriend. The woman screamed in terror, and her boyfriend appeared. A few phone calls later and a Key West police officer found the naked and rather drunk Tasker in the middle of the car park, and arrested him for disorderly intoxication and indecent exposure.

In the US state of Pennsylvania, attorney Wayne Johnson Sr was arrested for drunken driving shortly after leaving a court hearing in which he represented a client accused of drunken driving.

DOCTORS

In Norway, as part of the compulsory military service, people can be called back for refresher training later in life, and when one doctor received his papers he immediately swung into action to beat the call-up. The doctor, whose name was not made public, rubbed

An American doctor in the state of Oregon was jailed after he had sex with one of his patients, then charged the state health plan for the privilege. Dr Randall J Smith, 50, told the woman that the way for him to ease her pelvic pain was to massage certain trigger points. What with one thing and another, the massaging of those important trigger points led to sexual intercourse, and Smith also billed the Oregon Health Plan about £2700 for the 45-minute sessions. Nice work if you can get it.

ODD

sour cream into his hair. He poured liqueur onto his shoes. He slopped beer onto his clothes. He sat in his wardrobe and smoked 40 cigarettes one after the other. And for the two nights leading up to recall interview, he deprived himself of sleep. Then he spun the military a yarn about his life as a doctor having spiralled out of control, leaving him a boozy, stinking down-and-out. His ploy was successful – he was regarded as ineligible for service; but it was so convincing that after he left, the military doctor alerted the health authorities that this part-mad doctor was at large. This is when he became a victim of his own plan. The authorities ran checks against his name and saw the truth – that he was a well-respected professional consistently receiving high marks from his patients – with the result that he faced disciplinary action from both the health authorities and the military.

TEACHERS

The head of a school in the US state of Alaska took the highly innovative step of having himself disciplined for offences committed by his students. Steve Unfreid, principal of Matanuska Christian School, asked another teacher to whip him in front of two male students in the school's basement, after the boys were caught kissing girls in the locker room for the second time in a week. Unfreid told the students that he had to share in the discipline, took off his belt and asked teacher Joe Brost

law enforcers

The US military is constantly working to reduce the amount of cocaine smuggled out of Colombia, mainly by keeping a military presence there on anti-narcotics missions. Last year, though, four US soldiers were arrested on charges of drug trafficking, when their plane arrived in Texas from Colombia and was found to have 15 kg of cocaine concealed inside.

to whip him with it 'Like you would discipline your own son.' The idea was that the students were to stop the whipping when they acknowledged the gravity of their own crime. Unfreid was later sacked. Brost resigned. And the boys will probably carry on kissing the girls.

The consensual sex in the car was technically illegal, but the presence of a tot in the car added an element of tastelessness. A California high school teacher was accused of unlawful sexual intercourse with a minor, a 16-year-old student. And while she was having sex with the student in her own car, her two-year-old son was sitting strapped into the back seat.

Sport

The word sport derives from a meaning of 'having fun'. You wouldn't think so, though, the way poker-faced professionals approach their big-money, high-pressure jobs – but we've found some examples of that original meaning below.

Every year, it seems, wacky new sports are created: last year Britain's first 'urban golf' tournament was played on the streets of inner London. Played with a leather ball, urban golf uses buildings and telephone boxes with fire hydrant covers as the 18 holes. Sixty-three competitors and professional golfer Ronan Rafferty teed off on the 18-hole course in Shoreditch, east London, with each shot being played off a portable mat, just to make things a little bit fairer.

American golfer Bill Hilsheimer sank no less than three holes-in-one in a six-month period last year. Pretty amazing odds of that happening. But the odds go much, much longer when you realise that Bill, who lost most of his right hand in a childhood accident, plays golf one-handed.

More golfing weirdness from an impressively dedicated American who saw things on a grander scale. André Tolme of New Hampshire mapped out a golf course in Outer Mongolia that was 1300 miles long, and completed the first nine holes during 2003. He wintered in Russia and then finished his round in the summer of 2004 with a score of 12,170, not bad when you consider he only used a three-iron.

4

Sixty-three minutes into a Sunday league football match between Peterborough North End and Royal Mail AYL the referee reached for his red card – and sent himself off. Thirty-nine-year-old Andy Wain got involved in an incident after the Peterborough goalkeeper disputed a goal scored by AYL, and ref Wain lost his temper, threw down his cards, marched up to the loud-mouthed goalie and squared up to him. He then came to his senses and sent himself off, causing the match to be abandoned. 'It was totally unprofessional,' he said. 'If a player did that I would send him off, so I had to go.' Wain blamed his bad temper on the death of his father-in-law the day before the match, his wife being diagnosed with cancer, and then discovering just before kick-off that a friend had died of a heart attack.

DAFT

The director of a Thai prison wanted to stop his inmates from betting so much on football matches, and to switch over to actually playing in them. He decided to set up a football game against a team of outsiders, with a view to building up their self-esteem. The prisoners may have thought they would win easily when they saw that they were up against a team of elephants, but the match ended in a 5–5 draw because the elephants were specially trained in soccer. So much for the prisoners' self-esteem.

Professional footballers aren't always the brightest buttons, but this news snippet that came out last year really confirms it: the player liaison officer for Fulham FC, Mark Maunders, was called out to the home of star French midfielder Fabrice Fernandes, who had a problem that needed solving. Fernandes complained that he kept waking up with a wet head. A swift investigation revealed the simple facts that (1) his bedroom window was open and (2) it had been raining most nights.

STUPID

An interestingly weird Australian sport came to our attention last year – Goanna Pulling. Goannas are large lizards common in the Outback, as any Australian well knows, but the sport of Goanna Pulling, which was created in the New South Wales town of Wooli, is a one-on-one tug-of-war done lying face down, with a leather harness around each puller's neck. The object is to pull your opponent towards you across a line. (In doing so you apparently look a bit like a goanna.) At the National Championships the Luxton brothers, Clinton and Rhys, from Queensland took the heavy and middleweight divisions for the third year in a row.

GREAT SPORTING ACHIEVEMENTS

Weightlifting is an ancient and honourable sporting discipline – but generally using the arms to lift the weight. In the Chinese city of Harbin, however, a 55-year-old man lifted a 75 kg barbell for 10 seconds with his penis. The man, named Zhan, started out lifting small bricks, gradually adding weights as his manhood got stronger. He says his ability is really a form of kung fu, taught to him by his father to help him recover from an illness when he was a teenager.

Ilker Yilmaz of Istanbul belongs to that select group of athletes who can squirt milk out of his eye (he has to ingest some milk first, so it's not quite so weird that he also produces the milk). Yilmaz, who discovered his great talent while swimming, when he noticed that water that went up his nose emerged from the corner of his eye, due an abnormality in the tear ducts, decided to challenge Canadian Mark Moraal's 8.7 ft record for squirting milk. Here's how he does it: 'My technique is simple. I suck the milk into my nasal cavity, hold my nose, pull my left eyelid back with my finger, and squirt.' In October he sucked some milk up and pitched it 9.223 ft out of an eye socket in front of several witnesses. 'I'm happy and proud that I have put Turkey into the record books, even if it's only for milk squirting,' Yilmaz told a crowd in Istanbul, not forgetting also to mention his sponsors, the Kay Sut milk company.

Wei Mingtang, 55, a factory worker from the Chinese city of Guilin, made a bizarre discovery about his physical prowess when he was a young man. He found out that he could blow air out of his ears. He then came up with the idea of using them to inflate balloons with the aid of a pipe. And last year, at a spring festival party, Wei blew out 20 candles in a line within 20 seconds using a hose leading out from his ears.

Alfie Byrne became Britain's youngest ever karate black belt last year. How old was the tough little nipper when he passed the gruelling 90-minute test? Just six years old. Fortunately Alfie's dad, Ed, is a karate instructor, so he needn't be too intimidated by his little boy.

Food & Drink

We always have plenty of tasty food and drink stories for you to get your teeth into ...

A restaurant in the German city of Dresden put maggots on its menu, and has never looked back. The owner of Espitas, Alexander Wolf, added maggot ice cream, maggot salads and maggot cocktails to the restaurant's list and after a month found that they were fully booked for weeks and weeks. Wolf admitted he started cooking maggots for his diners as a bit of a joke, and the incredible success was a big surprise. Fried maggots with cactus and corn, paying homage to the maggots' home in Mexico, from where Wolf imports them, is another dish that can be enjoyed at Espitas, as well as maggots with chocolate sauce for dessert. Maggots are nutritious and extremely tasty, said Wolf, and with diners beating a path to his door, who are we to argue?

 The notorious durian is revered in south-east Asia as the 'king of fruits' for its soft and delicious flesh, and sometimes reviled by Westerners because of its unbearably pungent smell. The durian is also notable because it heats up the human body, causing the metabolism to go into overdrive. For this reason, last year a man in Thailand died shortly after feasting on a durian. Thavin Chaiya finished his durian, and immediately started calling for water. Then his eyes started bulging out of his head, and he fell to the floor in convulsions. He died on the way to hospital.

A British firm signed a contract with a Colombian company last year with a view to selling toasted Colombian ants. According to Todd Dalton of Edible Ltd, the toasted ants, known as big-bottomed ants, will be sold in Europe, Australia and the United States, and the taste is 'exciting and unusual'.

In Thailand, those who regularly enjoy the great taste of frog prefer the meat to be fresh. But after a surplus in the market, the frog farmers of the village of Bo Talo had to think quickly, and turned the surplus into canned frog. They were hoping the decrease in chicken and duck sales brought about by bird flu in south-east Asia would help their cause and that the food would hop off the shelves. **WEIRD**

How much would you pay for a burger? Maybe around £1 in a fast-food chain, maybe £5 in a more traditional restaurant? Well, if that's your budget, don't sit down at London's Zuma restaurant, where their beefburger is made with beef from Japanese 'wagyu' cattle, who live on rich diets that include plenty of beer, and who get regular massages to improve the texture of their flesh. Zuma's burger comes in a sesame seed bun with tomato, lettuce, gherkins, onions and mustard, and it will set you back a whopping £55. But you do get fries with it.

Meanwhile, as if to prove that London really is one of the world's most expensive cities, a very expensive soup went on the menu at Kai, a Chinese restaurant in Mayfair. It's a type of shark's fin soup called 'Buddha Jumps Over the Wall', it includes abalone, Japanese flower mushroom, sea cucumber, dried scallops, chicken, Hunan ham, pork and ginseng; it has to be ordered five days in advance and one bowl costs £108. Owner Bernard Yeoh reckoned he sold two bowls a month, and that it is well worth the money.

The Serbian town of Savinac attracted a swarm of chefs eager to compete in the World Testicle Cooking Championships. The contest winner was a plate of bull's and boar's nadgers served up by Belgrade gonad guru Dejan Milovanovic. An 'exotic' category is planned for next year, to include camel and ostrich testicles.

In Japan, a sweet has been marketed with a name that has somewhat upset priests at one of Japan's most famous temples. The temple is at Nara, in western Japan; it is famous for its giant Buddha statue, and the sweets that are sold by vendors around the temple go by the name of 'Snot from the Nose of the Great Buddha'. The packaging has a picture of Buddha picking his nose.

Who ate all the pies? The guests at the wedding of Huddersfield couple Stuart Booth and Joanne Robinson, that's who. And that's because the bride and groom opted for a three-tier, 50 lb wedding pork pie instead of the traditional cake. The mammoth pie – known as a 'wedding growler' – was baked and assembled by a three-man team over a 24-hour period at Hinchliffe's farm shop in Netherton, near Huddersfield, at the suggestion of the bride and paying tribute to the fact that her husband-to-be was a founder member of the Pork Pie Appreciation Society.

An Austrian chocolate maker last year joined forces with an Arabic camel farm to come up with a new contribution to the confectionery market – camel milk chocolates. Chocolatier Hochleitner developed the

Waiter, there's a fly in my noodles! Customer Li Juan, having her dinner in a restaurant in the city of Changsha, found a fly in her bowl of noodles, and demanded to see the manager. The waiter she was speaking to swiftly picked up the fly, popped it into his mouth and swallowed it. The restaurant then completely denied that anything unusual had been found in Li's dinner.

choccies using milk from a camel farm and dairy in the United Arab Emirates. Camel's milk is lower in fat and sweeter than cow's milk, apparently, and a production plant is planned to produce 50 tons of 'healthy and delicious' camel chocolate per month. The target market is wealthy customers of luxury hotels in Abu Dhabi and Dubai.

A Chinese man named Lu suffered both pangs of hunger and pangs of envy as he saw what one of his neighbours was having for his dinner. As Lu settled down

German police in the town of Wilster were called out to deal with a diner of quite incredible nerve. In response to a call from the owner of a Greek restaurant officers arrived to find a scene they had certainly never dealt with before: a 63-year-old man, trying to park outside the restaurant, had hit the accelerator rather than the brake, and had inadvertently reversed straight through the plate glass into the middle of the restaurant. The car had come to rest in front of a freshly laid table, so the man calmly sat down at it and ordered his dinner from bemused staff. After the police had taken down the man's details he carried on with his meal.

to a small plate of fried peanuts, his neighbour's dog was tucking into a succulent piece of freshly cooked pork shank. Lu's jealousy got the better of him and he tried to get the pork off the dog; but the dog wasn't prepared to give up his gourmet repast and bit Lu's hand severely enough for him to need hospital treatment.

DON'T EAT THAT, YOU DON'T KNOW WHERE IT'S BEEN

In Belgium, two directors of a meat wholesaler were arrested and 20,000 kg of meat were seized. The wholesaler supplied meat for hot dogs that were guzzled all around northern Europe, and those hot dogs were a little too genuine, since the meat seized turned out to have dog meat in it.

News emerged last year of a man in Kanpur, northern India, whose daily regimen includes a kilogram of grass. The man, named only as Gangaram, says that he can do without food if necessary, but not grass. Gangaram drew his inspiration from a Rajput ruler, Maharana Pratap, who survived on grass chapattis when hiding in the jungle during a war.

Science appeared to back up what every toddler instinctively knows when an Austrian doctor put forward the theory that eating your own snot is good for you. Dr Friedrich Bischinger claimed that dead bacteria in your nose-pickings have a positive effect on your immune system. So don't be bashful – munch that mucus.

A ten-year-old Italian boy from the town of Frosinone was put on a diet by doctors when he weighed in at 50 kg, but he failed to lose any weight. Not only that, but his parents noticed after a while that the family dog was looking a bit thinner than usual. They didn't put two and two together until the dog finally bit the boy, and they realised that he had been stealing the dog's dinner every day to offset his low rations.

A five-year-old boy reached into his breakfast cereal box for what he thought was a free toy and was terrified to see a two-foot-long snake emerge.

eating naughty meat

A Zambian man was arrested after police were alerted to the fact that he had gone to the grave of his dead grandson, dug up the body and started eating it. A hunter saw the man in a graveyard chewing pieces of flesh, which he had cooked in a pot. The police said they had no idea why the man had eaten part of his grandson.

and don't drink that either *

After violating an antisocial behaviour order that banned him from hanging around petrol pumps, Brian Taylor, 36, of Middlesbrough, ended up with a three-month jail sentence. Taylor had been filmed on CCTV on many occasions drinking and sniffing petrol, dancing around like a madman during the small hours of the morning, and slashing pump hoses to fill up his petrol can (which made for an interesting situation when customers tried to use a pump that had been slashed and found themselves sprayed with petrol). Taylor preferred to drink unleaded – the healthy option – but wasn't averse to a drop of diesel every now and then. Despite film footage to the contrary, Taylor denied ever drinking petrol. 'I'm daft, but I'm not that daft,' he said.

Jordan Willett, from Telford, sprinted out of the kitchen in a panic after the snake slithered out of the box of Golden Puffs. The manager of the local Netto supermarket, where the cereal was bought, launched an investigation into how the corn snake, which is native to Mexico and very placid, came to be in the cereal box.

EXPLODING FOOD

A highly explosive situation developed at a Norwegian mackerel canning factory last year. Food producer Stabburet heat-treats the cans to preserve the fish in tomato sauce, but a whole batch missed out. A short while later, with the fish starting to rot, there was a mass explosion as 1650 cans of extremely stinky mackerel and tomato sauce blew up, splattering the inside of the warehouse with decomposing fish and slimy sauce. The fact that in Norway this product is given the highly tasteless nickname of 'plane crash' (because of the combination of silvery fish and blood-red sauce) just adds to the general revolting impression.

More a case of food that just might explode, this one ... You hope your food doesn't go off, and in this case you really hope it doesn't go off – Olivia Chanes chewed on a hot dog she bought at a Costco in Irvine, California, and her teeth came into contact with something hard and metallic: a 9 mm bullet. Later, police checked the store's stock of hot dogs but no more bullets were found – until Olivia developed stomach pains and an X-ray at her local hospital revealed another hot-dog-based bullet, which she had already swallowed.

DRINK

A Russian oil company, Yukos, won a bizarre legal victory when a court ruled it could sell cannabis vodka. The court in the city of Voronezh dismissed a case claiming Yukos, and its billionaire owners, were promoting drug use by selling the vodka at petrol stations. Drug squad officers had seized a bottle of the vodka, which is made from hemp seed extract, but the court said the label on the bottle promoted vodka sales and not drug

Vimto may not be the best known **ODD** soft drink in the world – the cordial is a native of the city of Manchester and tends to be more popular in the north-west – but it inspires passion in its devotees. None more so than the Bird family of Timperley, near Manchester, who are so hooked on their favourite soft drink that they have a home supply of it hooked up on tap. A tank full of Vimto has been buried in their garden, with pipes leading to the kitchen so that they have a constant supply. When the tap is turned on, the cordial is pumped into a mixing chamber connected to the house's water supply. The Birds, Mandy and Clive and their two sons, get through 25 pints of the fruity drink a week.

use. It reads: 'Cannabis vodka – an alcoholic drink prepared from hemp seed extract. Try this wonderful drink, but don't forget its extraordinary powers.'

Unofficially made vodka is big business in eastern Europe, and cross-border smuggling is a big problem. Lithuanian border guards unearthed a three-kilometre pipeline for smuggling in moonshine vodka from neighbouring Belarus. The thin plastic pipe lay just a few centimetres beneath the surface of the ground and ran under several roads, along a riverbed and came to a halt next to the home of a Lithuanian resident. Other pipelines have been

Tea – best drink of the day, the cup that cheers. But in Assam, the heart of India's tea-growing industry, scientists have come up with a futuristic way of enjoying the drink – the tea pill. The secret formula was developed by technicians at the world's largest tea research facility, the Tocklai Experimental Station in Jorhat, Assam, and the pill can be sucked, chewed, put under the tongue or even dissolved in water and drunk. Whether people will start inviting each other in for a nice pilla tea remains to be seen.

discovered in the last few years, but this one was by far the longest.

Farmers in the Indian state of Andra Pradesh started ordering vast amounts of Coca-Cola last year – but not to drink and rot their teeth with. No, they started using it as a pesticide, partly because rumour has it that the fizzy pop works as well as a chemical pesticide, and partly because it is considerably cheaper than Nuvocron – 30 rupees for a 1.5 litre bottle of Coke as opposed to 10,000 rupees for one litre of Nuvocron. They use the Coke on their cotton and chilli crops.

Spiritual Life

Bridging the gap between heaven and earth…

Some priests are more in touch with what's going on than others … In Florida last year Jack Arnold, a Presbyterian minister, was delivering a sermon that included a quote from John Wesley about going to be with Jesus when your work on earth is finished. Arnold was halfway through a sentence that began 'And when I go to heaven …' when he collapsed and died.

Moving swiftly with modern times, a German church last year began selling mobile-phone ringtones with a slight difference. The St Petri church in Hamburg set up a website (www.petriklingel.de, if you're interested) to sell Christian ringtones, in order to help pay for the restoration of the church organ. For around £1.40, punters can download one of five hymn tunes, choosing from tunes that, as church musician Thomas Dahl said, have been popular for centuries.

A new website came to our attention last year, set up to help good Christians who are lapsing to stay on the straight and narrow: www.xxxchurch.com is dedicated to helping the faithful reject the addictive evil of pornography. For example, there is the NoHo section, where girls can take the pledge not to dress like a Ho ('I am discovering the joy of covering my butt cheeks and not showing so much skin'), and there is sound advice like 'Remain calm and tell yourself: "You don't own me, masturbation!"'

A Swedish pastor somehow succeeded in persuading his lover, who was also his family nanny, that she was receiving text messages from God. And worse, those text messages commanded her to kill the pastor's wife, which she did. Helge Fossmo, a Lutheran pastor, was found guilty of inciting Sara Svensson to murder his wife, and given a life sentence, while Svensson was placed under psychiatric care. Fossmo also used the text-message-from-God ploy to incite Svensson to shoot the husband of a former lover – but he survived the shooting. Svensson said that if she received messages from God instructing her to do something, and they really were from God, then she would have no alternative but to obey God's word. Unfortunately for Pastor Fossmo, though, the messages were traced back to his mobile phone rather than heaven.

✳

Here's a little tale of deceit backfiring on someone who should have behaved better. In Cambodia a Buddhist monk, Khong Chantha, sold a turtle that had Buddhist inscriptions carved into its shell to a woman for about £1. The woman started a little business with the turtle, saying it was magic and could help people by working miracles for them, and when Chantha found out he tried to take the turtle back off the woman by force. A fight broke out, and the woman reported the monk to the police, who found how he had managed to persuade the woman of the turtle's powers: he had a forged letter in his possession stating that he was a true reincarnation of the Buddha, and it was supposedly signed by the Cambodian president. Chantha was let off with a police caution. Maybe he should have got the magic turtle to help him.

STRANGE

A 24-year-old member of the Royal Navy became the first registered devil-worshipper in Britain's armed forces. Chris Cranmer, a technician aboard HMS *Cumberland*, was officially recognised as a satanist by the captain, after making a formal request to have his religion accepted, and giving a talk on his beliefs to the assembled crew, in accordance with Navy rules. His religion involves following nine satanic principles, including indulgence instead of abstinence, and vengeance instead of turning the other cheek. Cranmer became a practising satanist after reading Anton LaVey's *Satanic Bible* and realising that satanism was the perfect match for him. A Navy spokesman said: 'We are an equal opportunities employer.'

Animals

Animals could certainly teach us humans a thing or two about weirdness …

A Macedonian shepherd, Ordan Vandov, got talking to a local vineyard owner, who offered him some leftover grapes from the pressing process to feed to his sheep. The shepherd accepted, the sheep were fed the grapes, and after a while the two men finished their chat. The shepherd set off with his flock and

A Chinese man, apparently a hunchback, was stopped by a security guard as he boarded a plane in Guangzhou for a flight to Chongqing. The guard thought that the man's hump didn't look quite right, and he was correct – the man was trying to smuggle his pet turtle onto the plane by disguising it as a hump. The man said he knew live animals weren't allowed on the plane, but he was too fond of his turtle to leave it anywhere else. Eventually he checked the 5 kg turtle in as baggage.

WEIRD

immediately realised they were all drunk. The sheep were staggering around and some could barely walk. Vandov walked the five miles to the nearest town and hired a truck to drive the inebriated sheep home. Vandov had never seen anything like it, commenting that some of them couldn't even stand on their own four legs.

From drunken animals to a drunken owner of a weird pet: in the Russian city of St Petersburg, police received a call to say a brown bear was drifting on an ice floe on the Neva River. When they arrived at the scene and captured the bear, a man came up to them and announced that it was his bear. He said he had let it off the lead to play on the riverbank and it had climbed aboard the ice floe. He slapped a collar and lead on it (but no muzzle) and walked off, rather unsteadily, since he was clearly drunk.

A South African zoo was faced with the problem last year of trying to persuade its star chimpanzee to kick his smoking habit. Charlie, an adult male chimp living in the Bloemfontein Zoo, had been picking up cigarettes thrown to him by visitors and smoking them, aping the behaviour of the humans until he became addicted to the nicotine. A zoo spokesman said that Charlie had been showing the signs of a true nicotine addict, even acting like a naughty schoolboy by hiding

his cigarette when staff approached his area. The spokesman confirmed that the zoo was determined to help Charlie quit. It may be a big challenge: Charlie already has three bad teeth from drinking cans of soft drinks thrown to him by zoo visitors, and seems to have an addictive personality.

Hundreds of cows being transported from the US to the Middle East suffered a bizarre fate. Their high-protein diet meant that their flatulence was so potent and poisonous in the confined space that they gassed themselves to death.

Wildlife experts in Germany met with an inexplicable mystery last year as an epidemic of exploding toads swept the northern city of Hamburg. In scenes reminiscent of a sci-fi film, hundreds of toads swelled up and exploded over a period of a few days. Observers noted that the toads' bodies would reach about three and a half times their normal size as they swelled to their maximum limits, before bursting, hurling entrails about a metre. The peak time for the toads to trigger appeared to be between 2 am and 3 am, and veterinarians were at a loss to give an explanation for the phenomenon.

Landmines are a terrible problem in war-torn Mozambique, and detection is a priority. In the past sniffer dogs have been used, but one landmine-detection outfit switched from explosives-sniffing dogs to giant African hamster rats. It appears the lighter, more plentiful rats not only have noses that are just as sensitive, but they don't need as much affection and constant reassurance.

The Samek family, living in the Czech Republic, appear to have mastered the art of breeding very well-endowed rabbits. They managed to breed two rabbits that had two penises each, both bunnies eventually ending up in the cooking pot, but their masterstroke was to breed a bunny with three penises. The *Guinness Book of Records* refused their plea to register their bunny as a record, saying there was no category for multi-penised rabbits in the book. But just imagine how fast a three-penised rabbit would breed!

A parrot that seemed to be at death's door belonged to Marilyn King of Cumbernauld in Scotland. She became very concerned when her 13-year-old parrot, Nelson, began to wheeze and groan and cough, struggle for breath and ask for help in strangled tones. Medical tests pointed to the parrot being in good shape – then Ms King found out that Nelson used to live in an old people's home. Nelson was just imitating what he had heard all day. 'He does a great smoker's cough,' said Ms King.

Li Yong, from the Chinese city of Zhengzhou, bought a parrot and spent eight months trying to teach it to say 'Hello' and 'Goodbye', but the stubborn and contrary bird stayed completely silent. One day he lost his temper and shouted 'Idiot' (and a few other less printable things) at the parrot, who suddenly learned how to speak and repeated the insults to Mr Yong each time he walked by. Eventually Mr Yong cracked and strangled the parrot.

A case came up last year in the US capital, Washington DC, which revealed that the director of the city's zoo had obstructed a newspaper investigation into a spate of animal deaths at the zoo. The director had refused to release the medical records of one of the zoo's giraffes because, she said, she had to protect the animal's right to privacy.

Two tiger cubs received unusual attention in the Yangon zoo in Myanmar (formerly Burma). The cubs had to be removed from their aggressive mother for their own safety, and a local woman volunteered to breastfeed the stripy little darlings. Hla Htay only offered her services until the cubs' teeth grew, and suckled them four times a day for half an hour. Then they moved on to a bottle with a teat that was impervious to the pain of tiger teeth. **STRANGE**

IT'S A DOG'S LIFE

Two puppies stolen from a pet shop in the US state of Minnesota were recovered, but not quite in the same state as before. The little pooches had been dyed purple and blue by Sheila Hoffart, 19, who stole the shih-tzu and the sheltie pups, took them home and dyed their fur with her flatmate's hair colour. Hoffart then tried to sell one of the purple puppies but the purchaser realised it was one of the stolen pups and reported her. Hoffart had previously dyed two cats red.

This incident may have set alarm bells ringing throughout the French canine community: the birthright of every urban dog to pee up against a lamp-post was threatened. A man was walking his dog, a three-year-old Argentinian mastiff named Pako, in his home town of Wavrechain-sous-Denain in northern France. Pako felt the need, stopped at a handy lamp-post, cocked his leg and let fly. But there was a live wire loose and in contact with the metal post. Pako's urine completed an electrical circuit, Pako was jolted with a huge electric shock and he died on the spot. And his poor owner also received a shock when he tried to pick him up, and had to be taken to hospital.

When a New Zealand woman's baby stopped wanting to be breastfed, the mother decided her milk should go to her puppy. So Kura Tumanako, of the town of Hastings, plonked her Staffordshire bull terrier pup on to her tit twice a day and let him get on with it. Ms Tumanako's intent was that Honey Boy, as the puppy is called, will become particularly protective of her daughter. And may also follow large-breasted women around for no apparent reason.

There was much mischief at Battersea Dogs' Home last year as staff would come in in the morning to find dogs running wild and plenty of mess to clear up. Cameras were set up to find out how they were escaping, and it turned out that one dog, a lurcher named Red, had learned how to push back the bolt on his cage. When free, he would then go and release a load of

Poor old Attila Varga was ordered out of his flat in Cluj, Romania, because of the foghorn-like, wall-vibrating, neighbour-waking snoring of his dog. Sumo, a large Neapolitan mastiff, snored so loudly and resonantly that the walls of neighbouring flats shook violently. Attila shares his bed with his faithful hound, and had got so used to the snores that he no longer heard them.

A Turkish petrol attendant lost his mobile phone and assumed a customer had nicked it. Just in case he'd left it lying somewhere out of sight, however, he dialled his number from the petrol station telephone and was amazed to hear his dog's stomach start to ring. The naughty pooch had just picked it up and swallowed it. The next day, thanks to nature taking its course, he got his phone back, albeit less than perfectly clean.

playmates and the fun would begin, as food cupboards were ransacked and games of chase were played. Red didn't reckon on being spotted on camera, so the game was up and his kennel was made more secure.

Apollo the boxer dog started vomiting one day and refused to drink, at his home in northern Sweden, so his owner took him to the vet. There in the dog's stomach was a rubber duck that his owner remembered he had swallowed five long years ago. It had hardened and turned black, but it had not, as the owner had thought, dissolved over the years. The vet succeeded in removing the nightmarish little toy creature, and Apollo was back to normal, ready to swallow the next indigestible object.

UNPLEASANTNESS TO ANIMALS

A Canadian woman left her flat in the town of Windsor, Ontario, for a short while, with a young couple flatsitting for her. When the woman returned home she found first of all that the couple had left, leaving her flat in a right old state. Then, when she opened the fridge, she found the remains of her neighbour's cat. In a cooking pot. The flatsitting, catslitting couple were located by police, who deduced that the cat had been killed in the bath and hung from the shower before being converted into cat stew. While it is not illegal in Canada to eat a cat, animal cruelty is another issue, and police were pursuing that avenue with the couple.

 A 46-year-old woman was arrested for cruelty to animals in a very heavy metal rock 'n' roll kind of way – but Florida resident Cynthia Christensen seemed far from the stereotype. Wheelchair-bound Christensen was with a group of friends, one of whom had his pet python with him. Christensen asked to hold it, then bit its head off. Police were called, and she said a dog had done it, but there were eyewitnesses who had seen the grisly truth.

A police patrol in the German city of Nuremberg noticed a woman walking with her dog in the city centre. What struck them was how large and yet how dangerously thin the dog was. On questioning the woman, named only as Gerda M., police learned that she was trying to starve the dog down so that it could fit into her hand luggage on an aeroplane journey. The dog should have had a healthy weight of around 25 kg; when the police took it away from its owner it weighed less than half that, at 12 kg, and the dog's owner's goal was to get its weight down to 5 kg.

THE CALM BEFORE THE STORM

A slaughterhouse manager in China decided to make the last minutes of his clients' lives a little bit better. Guo Xianfeng, manager of an abattoir in Mainyang, has

Beijing hosts the 2008 Olympics – Shanghai last year hosted the Pig Olympics. Thousands of Shanghai residents crammed into a city park to watch a herd of pigs compete in races over hurdles, jumping through hoops, swimming and diving. The pigs are a midget species bred in Thailand that can be trained from an early age and who apparently love sport. 'I never thought a pig could be so clever,' commented one wide-eyed child.

BIZARRE

started seriously to pamper the pigs who visit his establishment, giving them showers, saunas and massages before they are electrocuted. Apparently the porkers fall into a relaxed slumber after such luxury and feel no pain when the electrocution takes place.

WHEN ANIMALS ATTACK

In some fields near Bargfeld, Germany, Jürgen Marwedel saw a friend driving by on a moped. The friend suddenly stopped and began to wave madly, signing at Jürgen to run over and help. A hare had attacked the rear tyre of the moped, biting into it and refusing to let go; and when Marwedel tried to pull the animal off, it turned its attentions to him, clamping its jaws on to his shoe, biting through it into his foot. The hare clung on with the same unshakeable tenacity so Marwedel had little alternative but to beat it to death with a stick.

A 23-year-old Serbian man fell asleep after a dip in a stream, with his lower body relaxing in a pool of cool water. He was woken by a sharp stab of pain in his groin, and found to his dismay that a large crayfish had gripped his penis with its pincers. A passing rambler heard his anguished cries for help and called the rescue services, who succeeded in making the crayfish loosen its vicelike grip on the man's member

A tourist in the Caribbean island of Guadeloupe was enjoying a swim when a needlefish (which, as you might imagine, has a very sharp, pointy snout) leapt from beneath the surface of the water and stuck itself into his eye. It then started to flap around, like a fish out of water, and eventually freed itself, but the damage was so severe that despite medical attention the man's eye could not be saved.

without any lasting damage. The young man took his revenge by taking it home and cooking it for his dinner.

Luke Tresoglavic was minding his own business enjoying his time snorkelling in the sea near Sydney, Australia, when a small shark attacked him. The shark sank its teeth into his leg, and just wouldn't let go. Without the merest hint of panic Tresoglavic swam a quarter of a mile to shore and got out of the water. Still the shark stayed clamped to his leg. He got into his car and drove to the lifeguards, who were astonished to see a man walk into their clubhouse with a small shark hanging grimly off his leg. Perplexed, the lifeguards tried to work out how to help Tresoglavic, and ended up hosing the fish with fresh water until it loosened its grip, leaving 70 puncture wounds below his knee.

And more fishy frenzy from Russia, where a woman did her son a favour by cleaning his fish tank. But what she thought were no more than 'well-fed goldfish' were in fact piranhas. The piranhas thought it was breakfast time as she reached into the tank to remove them, and attacked her hand, stripping the flesh off two fingers before she had time to shake her hand free. The woman required extensive surgery, and doctors said she was lucky not to have lost her hand. At least now she knows what piranhas look like.

Chef Matthew Stevens of Somerset opened a box of bananas and felt a sharp pain, as if he had stuck his hand on a thorn. But when he saw a large, unfamiliar spider crawling away and the pain grew and grew he knew something was amiss. Stevens had been bitten by one of the world's deadliest venomous spiders, the Brazilian wandering spider. Despite being in shock, Stevens had the remarkable presence of mind to take a picture on his mobile phone of the creature. Experts at Bristol Zoo were able to identify the spider and recommend the right antidote to the spider's venom when Stevens was taken to hospital, and his life was **saved**.

A horse race in Australia had to be abandoned when the jockeys were attacked by an angry flock of seagulls. During the 5.20 pm Goldenway Handicap at Sandown Races in Melbourne, the 12 riders were galloping down the home straight, on which a large flock of gulls was having a nice quiet sit-down. As the field roared towards them, they panicked and flew directly into the bunch of horses. Five riders were thrown and the other horses scattered across the course. One jockey suffered a broken arm, and the race was declared a 'no-race'.

Love, Sex & Marriage

Love has been described as 'temporary insanity'. Take away the 'temporary', and that's about right for these stories...

Only time will tell if this is a heartwarming story of persistence in love or a chilling tale of obsessive stalking ... a German woman met a lovely Danish chap in an Austrian ski resort, and after one dance with him she fell head over heels for him. She only knew his first name – Carsten – and didn't see him again during her stay. But she tracked him down after writing to 340 men named Carsten in the Copenhagen area, and she said that she would have written to the other 1100 Carstens too if she hadn't struck gold at number 340. What Carsten thinks about all this we do not know.

Another story emerged last year that shows the power of love to create weird obsessions, in this case one that lasted several years. Romanian Sandu Gurguiatu went to court in the town of Foscani to sue his former employer for unfair dismissal. But as soon

Where there's a will, there's a way, especially when it comes to sex-starved prisoners. Two Turkish prison inmates, convicted murderer Seylan Corduk, 40, and Kadriye Fikret Oget, 27, inside for planting a bomb in a market, drilled a 9 cm hole between their cells. Through this tunnel of love they managed to have sex, with the result that Oget got pregnant. The two secretive shaggers both received extra one-month sentences and fines for damaging public property.

as he set eyes on the judge, Elena Lala, he fell head over heels in love with her. Gurguiatu then proceeded to spend a small fortune on roughly a hundred pointless lawsuits just so he could get into court and see her. He managed to see her most weeks using this method, but Ms Lala was not interested – just sorry for him. Wonder why?

Lovesick? Or sick in the head, maybe? Charles Gonsoulin fell in love in an Internet chatroom and decided he just *had* to see his new sweetheart. Gonsoulin is from Los Angeles, where the sun always shines, and his lady love lived in the Canadian province of Quebec. Now Gonsoulin had a robbery conviction that prevented him from entering Canada, so he decided to cross the border on foot from the state of North Dakota, walking hundreds of miles and aiming for Winnipeg, where he hoped to get a bus to Montreal (a mere 1400 miles away). Oh, and it was slap in the middle of winter, things get mighty cold up there, and LA resident Gonsoulin had no experience of cold weather conditions. When the police caught up with the lovestruck fool after his long march through the Canadian winter, he was totally disoriented, suffering from severe frostbite that caused the loss of several fingers and toes. That didn't stop them from charging the 41-year-old with entering the country illegally, deporting him and preventing him from even meeting his new love. 'It was worth it for me,' Gonsoulin said afterwards, although we're not sure quite how.

Australia's Northern Territory awarded a $2500 grant for a series of three workshops for sex workers. The workshops in the city of Darwin, run by Mr Big Pants and Mistress Natasha (experts flown in from Brisbane), were on the subject of 'bondage discipline and sadomasochistic practice'. The workshops were a big hit, but local taxpayers weren't too happy when they found out where their money was going. Maybe they should visit the newly taught sex workers to learn how to accept a bit of pain.

First there's the argument; then one spouse (usually the wife?) says firmly to him or herself, 'No sex tonight.' Then the next day there's the kissing and making up. A court case in Sicily last year documented just such a denial of marital favours, by a husband, that lasted not for one night but for seven years. The man,

A Dorset man complained when the sex line he phoned, advertised as 'Hear Me Moan', turned out to be the tape of a nagging wife. But his complaint was overruled by Trading Standards, who pointed out quite reasonably that he got what he asked for. UNUSUAL

A Romanian shopkeeper got himself into big trouble with a group of women who complained that he was ruining their sex lives. Ion Barbu sold booze at all hours, and let customers have plenty of credit. Women in the town of Nistoresti said that their husbands were going out in the middle of the night to buy and drink booze, and that it was making many of the men impotent. They staged protests outside the store and complained to consumer protection officials, who closed down the store while investigations were carried out.

QUIRKY

named only as Francesco, got back at his wife, Piera, after she opposed him in a family argument, by withholding sex from her for seven years (you'd think she'd be grateful, but apparently not) and was ordered by the court to pay maintenance. The court called the man's behaviour an 'offence to her dignity' and said it constituted grounds for separation.

Paris's Père Lachaise cemetery is full of the graves of notable people, including nineteenth-century writer and journalist Victor Noir. Now Monsieur Noir had a reputation as a romantic figure, and the story goes that he was killed in a duel the day before he was to be married. The statue at his grave has a rather large bulge in the crotch, and over the years it has been the habit of women visitors to kiss the lips of the statue and give the groin a good rub, as a kind of fertility aid. But last year officials at the cemetery were forced to cordon off the statue in a bid to stop the 'indecent rubbing' and save Victor's statue from damage.

A straitjacketed teddy bear designed as a lover's gift for Valentine's Day and named 'Crazy For You' caused a bit of a stir in the US state of Vermont when it hit the shops. The bear, which was sold with madness-certification papers, was a big hit with shoppers, but drove mental health advocates quite mad. They called for the Vermont Teddy Bear Co. to withdraw the bears from the market because they were tasteless and stigmatised mentally ill people. Company president Elisabeth Robert disagreed, refused, and carried on selling the bears to love-crazy individuals in Vermont.

MARITAL MADNESS

The miserable story of the marriage of Scott McKie and Victoria Anderson was told at Manchester Crown Court – a sign in itself that it hadn't gone that well. But that is an understatement: the marriage lasted about one and a half hours and disintegrated in a flurry of violence at a pub in Stockport where the reception was held. Twenty-three-year-old Scott McKie got into trouble quite early on in the marriage – at this reception, during his toast to the bridesmaids, in fact. He said something a little off-colour (quite what, we do not know), to which 40-year-old Victoria Anderson took great exception. In a rage she took a large ashtray and hit her new husband over the head. McKie picked up a hatstand and hurled it, javelin-style, at the bar. Police were quickly called and McKie immediately took up the challenge, headbutting one of the officers and punching another. As he was dragged off to the cells, his new wife cancelled the honeymoon and instigated divorce proceedings.

A Romanian man was fed up with his wife's constant gossiping and chatting with her friends, so he took a very unusual course of action. Puiu Dobrica, from Andreiasu, waited until his wife Aurelia went into their pigsty to clean it one morning, and then locked the door from the outside. Mrs Dobrica spent a whole day and night in the pigsty until her son released her the next morning. Mr Dobrica, a barber, said afterwards that he didn't see anything wrong with what he did: after all, he did take the trouble to feed her twice through a hole in the roof.

A Serbian woman, Vinka Mijovic, 32, from Garas, was furious when her wealthy fiancé Miodrag Tomovic, 68, inconsiderately died before he could marry her. So she invested some of her money (assuming she would inherit plenty) in bribes: she bribed a local registrar to sign a marriage certificate saying the couple had turned up for the wedding, and she bribed two friends to be the best man and a witness to the wedding. Then two weeks after Tomovic's death, she announced it and tried to get a lawyer to turn his fortune over to her; but relatives complained to the police; the dead man's signature was found to have been forged and Ms Mijovic went to jail for 18 months.

An Egyptian professor discovered on his wedding night that his beautiful young bride, whose seductive mane of hair had attracted him to her, was bald. The professor admired her as she slept and couldn't resist running his fingers through her locks – at which point her wig came off in his hands. Not only did he file for divorce, but also claimed damages of more than £50,000 for deception. The woman had lost her hair after an illness at a young age and had worn a wig ever since.

A Chinese couple in their eighties had been happily married for decades until one day – well, you know how it is when something's been on your mind for a while – the husband went out and had a sex change operation, returning home an elderly woman. His wife made an effort to carry on living with him as a sister, but couldn't deal with it, so they divorced.

An Iranian woman, named only as Mina, last year asked for a divorce from her husband. She was kicking up a stink about the fact that he stinks – he had not washed for over a year. At the beginning of their eight-year marriage her husband was very clean indeed, showering three times a day and regularly washing his hands. Then suddenly everything changed, and his near-obsessional washing was transformed into near-obsessional avoidance of water. Over a year later, no one in his family or at work could bear to be near him, and Mina filed for divorce. But she'll be lucky to get one – it is very hard for a woman to obtain a divorce in Iran, even if your husband is a soap-shy stinker.

A woman in the United Arab Emirates was married for no more than one day when she had the knot untied after discovering her new husband was deaf and dumb. The couple had met only once before, when his relatives put his apparent reluctance to utter a word down to chronic shyness.

When 38-year-old Chinaman Jian Feng's wife gave birth to their baby he was less than ecstatic. He considered the baby to be extremely ugly, whereas his wife was extremely pretty – that was one of the reasons he had married her, after all, after a whirlwind romance just two years earlier. He leapt to the conclusion that she had slept with someone else, but she 'fessed up to having had plastic surgery before her marriage and showed him an old photo of herself in her ugly days. Feng successfully won his divorce case against her for 'deceit'.

For some deeply stupid reason – maybe he was blinded by love – an Israeli man taught his pet parrot the name of the woman he was having an affair with. When the man's wife heard the parrot greeting her with a strange name she hired a private detective to investigate. The detective did his job well: he snapped some pictures of the man in a compromising position with his lover – with the blabbermouth parrot also in the shots. Next stop, the divorce court.

A Romanian man, Vladut, from the town of Constanta, fell in love with compatriot Elena during a trip to France, and they agreed to meet up again when they were both back home in Romania. Elena backed out, though, because she had had an accident and wanted time to get better, and sent her identical twin sister Monica in her place. The unsuspecting Vladut immediately proposed to the person he thought was the woman of his dreams – and Monica accepted. She didn't say who she really was and they were married for three years before the secret came out. Vladut demanded a divorce and Monica agreed, so he will eventually be with the right woman.

Two lonely souls looking for love met in an Internet chatroom. Slowly, hesitantly at first, love grew for the two Jordanians Adnan and Jamila. The two lovers were soon making plans to spend the rest of their lives together and eventually decided to meet in the flesh at an anonymous bus station north of the capital, Amman. Adnan's real name was Bakr, and Jamila's real name was Sanaa, and when they met they saw that each had

A Saudi man and his wife arrived at Bisha airport in the south of Saudi Arabia for a flight that turned out to be repeatedly delayed. He wanted to go back and get another flight on another day, while she insisted on being patient and staying at the airport. By 11 pm the husband had completely lost his patience with his wife – and, as allowed by Saudi law, divorced her on the spot. **WEIRD** fallen in love with their spouse – Adnan and Sanaa had been separated for a few months – and had been planning to marry someone they didn't actually like that much. Adnan solved matters in the traditional Islam way by shrieking, 'I divorce you,' three times, officially ending their marriage and giving them both a chance to find love again in an Internet chatroom.

The Reverend Brian Statham was shocked when Sonia Wilde made an unusual request for her wedding at St Matthew's Church in Edgeley, Stockport. She asked if her best friend, Lucy, could be her bridesmaid – Lucy being not only her best friend, but also her dog. The Rev. Statham finally agreed, and Sonia got down to designing a nice dress for Lucy to wear for the ceremony.

So close to the magic century, and yet so far ... An Indian man with his heart set on marrying a hundred wives died last year nine short of the ton. Udaynath Dakhinaray, 84, had first married young, while still a student, and when the marriage broke up vowed to take a hundred wives, but his total never got past 91. That's 90 more than many people, so nothing to be ashamed of. **ECCENTRIC**

NAG, NAG, NAG

A German man from the town of Itzehoe faced the choice of a £55 parking fine, or, if he didn't cough up the money, ten days in jail. Imagine the shock for the local police force when the 47-year-old man rang up and asked to be picked up from home for his ten days of porridge. He said that he was sick and tired of his wife's nagging and bickering, and a quiet little stint in prison, away from the trouble and strife, was just what he needed.

A man from eastern India, Enadul Mullick, had really had enough of his wife's nagging. The grocery store owner was forever getting slaughtered by his wife, Halima, for how little money he earned. One day he saw the darkest shade of red, fetched a cleaver, dragged his wife into the kitchen and chopped off the nagging tongue. Mullick admitted his crime to police, while his wife was in hospital where doctors were desperately trying to reattach her tongue (so she could start nagging him again when she got out of hospital).

In Iran, a woman took her husband to court to secure a judicial order for him to beat her just once a week instead of every night. The woman, identified as Maryam J, said that her husband had shown no signs of giving up his once-a-day habit of giving her a hiding, but that she wasn't looking for a divorce, just some respite. Acknowledging that her husband's violence was 'in his nature', she merely asked the judge to make her husband promise to beat her no more than once a week. The husband told the judge that a daily beating only commanded respect from a woman, but the judge made him sign a written assurance that he would stop altogether.

A Romanian woman, Mariana Schuster, was obliged by her husband to sign a legal contract when he received a life sentence for murder. The agreement he drew up was that she should be faithful to him for the duration of his stay in prison, probably 30 years, and in order to make sure she was, she must not leave the house during that time. Well, it emerged last year that 46-year-old Mrs Schuster had stayed true to her word for 15 years, and had not left the house at all. In those 15 years her sisters-in-law have looked after her, and she told local press that she wasn't at all lonely.

IT'S OVER BETWEEN US ...

Hypnotist Paul McKenna, one of the UK's best-known entertainers, was dumped by his girlfriend – on live TV. Ex-model Liz Fuller texted him, reminding him to tune in to her show on *Auction World*. During a sale of

You give up your own kidney for the man you love, and what do you get? John Jewell, 53, of Berkshire, left his wife, Carol, after 33 years of marriage, to move in with Carol's brother's wife. And all that after Carol had donated a kidney to her sick husband when it was found that she was a perfect match as a donor. John gratefully received the kidney, but decided that Carol was no longer the perfect match for him and kicked her into touch, running off with Marilyn Edmeades, Carol's sister-in-law. It was a case of take the kidney and run.

engagement rings – oh, the irony – she turned to camera and announced that she was leaving her boyfriend. 'Going, going, gone,' she said, 'like you!'

Rebecca Roberts was dumped by her partner of six years, Matthew Barratt, in rather weird circumstances. The couple, from Burnham in Somerset, had a young son, but that didn't stop Matthew from running away to Ohio in America to be with a woman he had met over the Internet. Matthew's new love was a woman known to him as Akasha, and she was in charge of a blood-worshipping cult – in fact she styles herself a vampire. After 'meeting' Akasha online,

Police in Chile were on the look-out for a very sore loser who left his girlfriend just as sore. The teenager, from the town of San Fernando, was told by his girlfriend that she was ending their relationship, so he asked for one last farewell kiss. He then bit off her lip and spat it out onto the ground before running away. Ironically she had decided to dump him partly because he was a bad kisser.

Matthew started shaving off all his body hair, dressing in black and using Rebecca's lipstick to redden his eyes (he could have bought his own lipstick, don't you think?). He also adopted a vampire name, Mathau. One day he swore total allegiance to Akasha, left a note for Rebecca saying he had to go, and disappeared to live his vampire life elsewhere.

TILL DEATH NEARLY DO US PART

Two days before their wedding, Katrina Grant, 36, from Warwickshire, confessed to her 22-year-old fiancé Luke Grant, that she felt he was too possessive, and that maybe the marriage wasn't a good idea. Then, not wanting a big argument, she went to bed. Luke went to the kitchen, took an eight-inch knife, went upstairs and stabbed her, puncturing her lung. A month later, while Luke was out on bail, they were married. 'He's worth a second chance,' said Katrina. Of course he is – just don't ever make him angry.

How's this for synchronicity? A Chinese woman in the city of Chengdu accidentally tumbled from the balcony of her fifth-floor flat, hitting an awning and a power line on the way down to the ground. Meanwhile, her hubby was on his way back from the cigarette shop

An Italian metal worker tried to kill his wife using a bizarre home-made gun disguised as a pair of crutches. Silvano Angelini shot his wife as she arrived at court in Siena for a hearing – the two were separated, and Angelini had arrived earlier pretending to be handicapped, hobbling around on his crutches. As his wife approached, he moved towards her, raised one crutch and fired, wounding her with the 12 mm barrel he had built into one of the crutches. Luckily, police were close by and disarmed Angelini, whose other crutch also had been converted into a gun and was ready to fire another shot.

UNUSUAL

and was just at the bottom of the block of flats when he saw her fall. He rushed forward and positioned himself so that he caught her. Both the husband and wife, who had just had an argument, were fine.

David Masenta and his fiancée, Mgwanini Molomo, of the South African village of Ceres, had a big argument, just a month before Mgwanini was due to give birth to David's child. It must have been one hell of a row, because David first shot and killed Mgwanini, then turned the gun on himself. When the tragic couple were discovered by family, it was decided to remember them as a 'happy couple, destined for a happy life together' and a marriage was swiftly arranged. As one cultural expert commented before the wedding: 'This does not mean the relationship has irretrievably broken down.' The groom's corpse was dressed in a smart suit, his bride-never-to-be in a wedding gown and a priest blessed the union. And then they were buried.

OLD FOLKS

Older and wiser? Not necessarily …

How to fill the long, lonely hours when you are in the twilight of your life? An 80-year-old woman in Austria tried to alleviate the boredom by staging a spoof bank robbery. Brandishing a toy pistol, she threatened a cashier at her local bank, told the cashier that it was a stick-up, and burst out laughing when she saw the expression of terror on the cashier's face. Later, in court, she told the judge she had only done it for a laugh, and received a three-year suspended prison sentence. The judge also mentioned that if she reoffended in that three-year period she would not get off so lightly – the woman pointed out she might not live that long anyway.

Patricia Tabram, 66, of Northumberland, loves cooking. She bakes biscuits and cooks soups and casseroles for herself and friends. The crucial difference between Mrs Tabram and other grandmothers-

of-two who enjoy spending time in the kitchen is that she laces it all with liberal helpings of cannabis. What's more, she has written a book called *Grandma Eats Cannabis*, which she hopes will soon make it to the nation's bookshops. Mrs Tabram, who suffers from whiplash pain and depression, which have been much eased by her regular diet of cannabis, has appeared in court after admitting possessing the drug with intent to supply.

And for those in the twilight of their lives who still want to burn brightly, a visit to Holland is in order. The Zierikzee Residential Home for old folks had what the residents called a 'bounce room' built into it. The room has a double bed, a fireplace and a bottle of wine provided with the booking fee. The aged residents do not have to be married to use the room, which has been set up to provide the 150 residents with the opportunity to indulge in some intimacy in a secluded spot, rather than the back of the TV lounge, for example. And inviting prostitutes in is within the rules, too.

In the US state of Virginia 75-year-old Jane Fromal ran herself a bath and got in. She wanted a good long soak, but she hadn't planned on soaking for five whole days. She had run the bath because she had a sore back, which was why she was unable to get herself up out of the water. A neighbour noticed newspapers piling up in her doorway and relatives found Fromal sitting in the bath, having survived by drinking water from the tap. Her first request on being freed after five nicotine-free days was for a cigarette.

Police in the Essex towns of Clacton-on-Sea and Frinton-on-Sea started a scheme to help old-age pensioners in the war against crime, in the shape of cat bells. Tinkly little cat bells have been given out to pensioners to put on their purses, so that they can hear if their purse is being snatched. A police spokeswoman said thefts had halved since the bells were introduced, but a council leader described the scheme as an insult to their intelligence.

Vulnerable pensioners now have devices other than cat bells at their disposal to protect them from almost any sort of danger. Sixty-two-year-old Serb Miladin Nikolic was so sick of being attacked by dogs when out walking in his home city of Belgrade that he

Last year we brought you the heartwarming story of Kimiani Maruge, an octogenarian Kenyan who finally made it to primary school after a lifetime of tending cattle. Well, he was back in the news again, but this time because he is facing expulsion from the school for 'disruptive behaviour'. Parents of other pupils have protested to the headmistress that great-grandfather Mr Maruge demands all the teachers' attention, and distracts them from learning. So even though Mr Maruge came top of the class last year, his school career may be short-lived. Maybe next year we'll be able to update you on this story again.

WEIRD

A Chinese woman in her seventies was given a lovely joke present by her 11-year-old grandson, to mark Teachers' Day, but it had more than the desired effect. The old woman, an ex-teacher, unwrapped her gift to find a plastic severed head; she suffered a stroke brought on by shock, and died shortly afterwards. And the poor lad had spent all his pocket money on it.

developed a protective walking stick. The stick is equipped with two retractable blades and fires blank bullets; it has a watch, a thermometer and a compartment for an address and phone number, while the deluxe version also sports a panic button and a loud 'bang' noisemaker. 'You should see the dogs run when I come down the road now,' he said.

South African authorities finally stepped in to enforce the burial of a man whose family were convinced that he would be resurrected. When 77-year-old Paul Meintjes died, his body was kept in his wife's bedroom because the family had been told by a 'prophet' that he would be resurrected on a certain date. After three days the smell from the corpse was so bad that officials declared it a health risk, and it had to be removed to the local morgue. Several weeks passed, during which time the body lost whatever freshness it had ever had, and all the prophet's resurrection dates came and went; eventually the police obtained legal permission to bury the corpse themselves. No details about the 'prophet' were available other than rumours that he was a former bank manager.

Old folks are entitled to a bit of exaggeration about their exploits earlier in their lives, but this one beggars belief. Ninety-year-old Ben Gale claimed last year that when he lived in California back in the 1970s he invented the phrase 'Have a nice day.' 'It spread like wildfire,' said Mr Gale. Of course it did, Ben ...

DEATH

Death is part of life. So are stupidity and weirdness...

A Romanian woman showed a keen, if macabre, eye for business, when she made a bit of money from her dead husband. The woman, from the town of Critesti, removed her husband's remains from his grave and then sold the burial plot. Her late husband's family were more than a little upset, but the woman pointed out that he was her husband, she had lived with him for 20 years and it was her choice; although dumping what was left of his body just outside the cemetery doesn't seem that respectful. The man's family recovered his remains and had them reburied in a different cemetery.

Two macabre death rituals were reported last year in India, both taking place about the same time. In the first, in West Bengal, a group of worshippers dug up three freshly buried bodies, decapitated them and offered the heads to Lord Shiva. The ritual would have remained secret had not the daughter of

In the US state of Wisconsin, Karen Stoltz faced a court hearing last year for a weird crime she committed over ten years earlier. Stoltz's boyfriend at the time, Michael Hendrickson, died in 1992 from a self-inflicted gunshot wound, and his ashes were buried in a cemetery plot. But just over ten years later, when relatives visited the plot, they discovered that not only were the ashes no longer there, but cans of beer and cigarettes that had been buried with him had also been taken. It seems that Stoltz had taken the remains not long after the burial ceremony, smoked the ciggies and drank the beer. When detectives went to her house, they found the ashes still in her garage.

one of the deceased complained to police that her father's body had been exhumed and beheaded for the rituals. In the same area, a crowd of about 1000 witnessed a procession of worshippers carrying the impaled, blood-soaked head of a child whose body had been removed from a burial ground shortly after it had been laid to rest.

THE STUFF OF NIGHTMARES

A Swedish woman took a photograph of a beautiful swan on the frozen river outside the royal palace in Stockholm, and got the shock of her life when the film was developed and she looked more closely at the picture: next to the swan there was a human hand sticking out of the ice. Marita Larsson reported her gruesome find to the Stockholm police, and a spokesman said the hand might be that of a man who committed suicide in the middle of winter and whose body had not been found.

A murder victim left a clue to his killers' identity written on his hand. The dead body of Francisco Lopez, shot in the US city of Dallas, had a set of numerals written on the back of his hand. Lopez had noticed a car cruising suspiciously around near his home and noted down the number plate on his hand because he thought the occupants were thinking of stealing his

feeding the animals

An Indian farmer made a bizarre request concerning his own death. New World Laldingliana, 46, wrote a will instructing that he wants his remains to be eaten by animals after his death. Mr Laldingliana, from the state of Mizoram, registered his will at a magistrates' court in the state capital Aizawl, reportedly stating: 'I, New World Laldingliana, have decided to give my body to wild animals when my life on earth is over to show that I had given my life for them. One of my greatest wishes is to throw a feast for the wild animals in Phawngpui forest with my own body.'

Cadillac. He saw the car again the next day, confronted the men inside and was shot dead. Police noticed the numbers as they looked over the body of 18-year-old Lopez, traced the car and two men were arrested and charged with murder.

CAN'T LIVE WITHOUT YOU

Canadian couple Helen and Bill Wilson met as teenagers in the 1920s, and married during World War II, embarking upon a marriage that lasted 63 years. In later years they moved into a care home, and, at the age of 94, Bill went down with flu and was taken to hospital. The same night he went in, Helen was at the home with her son, Jack, and suddenly started talking about Bill in the past tense. She went to sleep and died shortly afterwards in her sleep. The next morning, Jack went to see his dad and found him in a slightly delirious state, and was unable to tell him that his wife had died – but Bill asked Jack to get a chair for his mother because he could see her standing in the doorway. Unaware that his wife had died, Bill passed away shortly afterwards too, the couple dying within a day of each other.

In no way was German inventor Jürgen Bröther taking advantage of the grief of those mourning the loss of their loved ones when he introduced his 'telephonic angel' system. It's a battery-operated, underground loudspeaker buried by the grave that allows someone to speak to their dear departed ones through a microphone, with the messages amplified through the earth. At around £1000 per unit, it's great value. And the battery lasts for a whole year.

WEIRD DEATHS

Garlic is good for you. Try telling that to the Chinese warehouse workers in Zhengzhou city who died when shelves stacked 10 metres high with garlic collapsed onto around 30 workers, killing 15.

 An Austrian council worker met his untimely and remarkable end when his lawnmower ran over a

Charisse Hartzol of Chicago was struck by two events: the death of her aunt, and then a dream that warned her of her own death. Actually make that three things that struck Ms Hartzol, because straight away after her premonition she set off at dawn from where she was working to get to a church in Chicago as quickly as possible and pray, but was killed in a head-on car crash.

STRANGE

discarded shotgun cartridge. The cartridge exploded, igniting the lawnmower's petrol tank and sending the poor chap flying backwards through the air, and the lawnmower landed on his head killing him instantly.

A freak accident turned a fire extinguisher into a deadly weapon at a workshop in New Zealand. Tracy Uhlenberg was killed instantly when the fire extinguisher fell onto the floor and began to discharge pressurised gas from a damaged valve. Like a balloon that has been blown up then allowed to deflate, the fire extinguisher took off violently, shooting across the workshop, breaking a worker's ankle, then left the ground like a rocket, hitting Mrs Uhlenberg on the head before smashing through the workshop wall at a height of six metres.

'Eat my shorts,' says Bart Simpson from time to time. And since edible knickers have been around for some time now, that isn't as dangerous a thing to do as you might think. But it all went badly wrong for Jean-Louis Toubon, of Marseille, when munching on his girlfriend's succulent smalls – some pieces of her knickers got stuck in his throat and he choked to death.

In Egypt, meanwhile, seven workers met a very bizarre death when they drowned in a vat of animal blood. One worker fell into the vat, at an abattoir near the Red Sea port of Aqaba, and each subsequent worker died jumping in to save the one before. The farm manager said that the blood was clotting, which made it extremely difficult to swim in.

Lorry driver Juliano Parker's first misfortune was when a front tyre and brake drum fell off his lorry on the M62 in Yorkshire. His second, and fatal, was when he went onto the grass verge to haul it back; the tyre exploded in his face, killing him instantly.

Two pilots for a regional airline in the USA, Pinnacle Airlines, were flying with no one else on board, and told air controllers they were taking the aeroplane to its highest possible altitude – 41,000 feet – in order to have a little fun, as they said. But what followed was far from fun. As the aeroplane reached 41,000 feet, the engines failed. And that was it. The pilots tried unsuccessfully to restart the engines and plummeted to their deaths.

WEIRD

Liliana Ruffini was visiting her family's private crypt in northern Italy as part of preparations for the burial of her brother the next day. Unfortunately Mrs Ruffini didn't see that a marble slab in the mausoleum had been removed and fell into a ten-foot-deep hole to her death. It would have been tempting just to leave her there, wouldn't it, seeing as it was more or less where she would end up anyway.

BREAKING UP IS HARD TO DO

Every year people hang on for just too long a time. Learn to let go!

 In Japan police discovered last year that three elderly siblings had been living with their father's decomposed corpse for nearly a decade. Kyujiro Kanaoka's body was found on a bed at the family's home in the city of Itami in western Japan. His children, all aged over 70, told police they had thought their father was still alive for all that time, and only recently had it occurred to them that he might possibly be dead.

In a remote area of the US state of Wisconsin, Philip Schuth became involved in a police siege after he shot a neighbour. When he eventually surrendered, a bizarre story unfolded: Schuth's mother, Edith, had died in 2000, and he had kept her body in his freezer while he collected her social security money to live on. Schuth didn't tell anyone when she died, he said, because he thought that he would get the blame for her death. Several years earlier, she had been attacked by a cat in the house, it seems, and the fact that there were several drops of her blood on the walls made him think he'd be charged with her murder. When police opened the freezer, they found the body of his mother, sitting up, and surrounded by mounds of ice. What is a little weird is that he didn't even need to keep her body in order to get her social security money, because it was paid directly into a bank account every month. What was also weird was the collection of home-made bombs, sawn-off shotguns and other guns that police found inside the house.

SUICIDE STORIES

A double whammy: in northern China a woman tried to end her life by jumping from the block of flats she lived in with her husband. He was in front of the block when he saw her climb out of the window, and ran to try and break her fall. He succeeded in one sense, in that she did land on him, but the collision killed both of them.

In the US state of Utah, police were called to a man's house to stop him slitting his wrists. While they were there, officers found the man's mother sitting in a car in the garage trying to kill herself using the exhaust fumes.

A Taiwanese man leapt to what he thought would be his death from the 23rd floor of an office block, but landed on a parked car. In the car was a woman, waiting to pick up a friend. She, poor thing, was killed by the impact, which broke her neck, whereas the would-be suicide survived with a cut face and a broken leg.

We've featured weird home-made equipment before in this grisly section, and here is another example: a 74-year-old Lithuanian man built his own electric chair to end it all. When relatives in his home town of Kaunas, concerned that they had not heard from him for a long time, broke into his flat, they were faced with the sight of him still seated in his chair, rigged up with electrodes, and wires plugged into the wall socket.

In Scottsdale, in the US state of Arizona, the city's finance director, aged 55, climbed out of his car while driving at about 50 mph, got up onto the roof, stood with his arms wide open, then jumped, skidding along the ground and hitting a tree with lethal force. Kevin Keogh was pronounced dead at the scene. But it is almost certain that Keogh was not suicidal, despite so clearly bringing about his own death. A few years earlier, while travelling in Mexico, he picked up a rare parasite that slowly damages the brain, in particular the frontal lobe; in non-scientific terms the effect is to make you want to do crazy things, like jumping out of your car at 50 mph.

In the US state of Oregon, Gerald Krein was charged with 'solicitation to commit murder and conspiracy to commit manslaughter' after he was tracked down as the organiser of an Internet suicide pact planned for Valentine's Day. Krein set up his group of would-be suicides via an Internet chatroom, attracting mainly women, including a mother who also planned to kill her two children. According to the authorities, Krein planned to coordinate the suicides over the Internet using webcams, but the plot was exposed when one of the 'Suicide Party 2005' group lost her nerve, and informed the police. Other members came forward and added the information that the mass suicide was to have taken place by hanging. The chatroom was closed down immediately.

The ultimate sacrifice? Maybe not in this case. In the Indian city of Chennai, a mother committed suicide so that her two blind sons could receive the corneas from her eyes and see. Thirty-seven-year-old Tamizhselvi's sons, Kumaran, 17, and Kumar, 15, were both born blind, but doctors were very doubtful that their mother's sacrifice would be of any use, since neither case of blindness was definitely curable with a cornea transplant. The family nevertheless insisted that Tamizhselvi's corneas could only be used for her sons and no one else.

SPECTACULAR FAILURES

In California, a woman called police to say that her son had a shotgun and was about to kill himself. As soon as the police arrived at their house, he ran off into some woods to carry out his threat, but crisis negotiators called him on his mobile and started trying to make him reconsider. Then the situation was turned bizarrely on its head: the man rang the authorities back from his hiding place to say he had just been bitten by a snake and please could he have medical treatment. The man was taken in, treated and then charged with brandishing a firearm.

A 39-year-old man in the US state of Ohio had three goes at ending his own life, all gas-based and all

A 32-year-old Czech man failed to kill himself when he tried to hang himself from a tree; the branch broke under his weight and fell to the ground, breaking both legs, which was not quite what he wanted. When he came out of hospital he had another go, using a method he was certain would do the job. He took a chainsaw to his throat, but, incredibly, the blade missed his jugular and stuck in his spine. Not dead, but badly injured, it was back to hospital ...

unsuccessful. First he ran a hose from his car's exhaust into the car, but his car ran out of fuel before he succumbed. Later he hooked up a propane gas tank in the same way, and once again the gas ran out before his life did. Finally, and most ironically, he turned on the gas at home to kill himself, but realised that he might be endangering other people's lives and ran to the cellar to turn off the electricity. As he did so his fears were realised: an electrical spark ignited the gas, his house was blown to pieces, and neighbouring houses suffered heavy damage, while the man ended up in hospital.

This story sounds almost like the script for a Coen Brothers film – gruesome and with macabre twists. In Melbourne, Australia, a man wanted to end it all, but was too scared to go through with it. But instead of wasting time trying to pluck up courage, he threw money at the problem in the weirdest of ways – he took out a contract on himself. The 30-year-old man hired two young men from Melbourne's underworld, at A$5,000 each, to kill him. Plan A was this: he would take an overdose of sleeping pills, the two hitmen would check him for signs of life ten minutes later, and if he wasn't dead, they were to kill him with an iron bar. So they drove out from Melbourne into the hills of Gembrook to find a convenient cliff where they could dump the future corpse, but nothing suitable could be found. At this point the man proposed Plan B, which was that he would still take the overdose, but his body would be hidden in some bushes. Two boxes of pills later, the man fell into a deep coma, but began to convulse on the ground. Since this clearly meant he wasn't dead yet, the two hitmen kept their side of the bargain and whacked him over the head a few times with an iron bar, then departed, satisfied that they had done their job. However, the man was far tougher than anyone imagined: not only did the overdose not kill him, neither did the blows to the skull. He eventually regained consciousness and was later found staggering down a road – in a bit of a state, blood everywhere – and was taken to hospital. Police caught up with the two men, who made full confessions, having conspicuously spent much of the A$10,000 on Cuban cigars, expensive liquor and mobile phones.

And if you thought the previous story was weird, try this one. An English teenager posed as a secret agent in an Internet chatroom in order to persuade a friend to stab him to death. 'Skilled writers of fiction would struggle to conjure up a plot such as that which arises here,' said the judge at Manchester Crown Court, where the case was heard. The 14-year-old boy, named only as B, managed to convince Boy A, aged 16, that he had been recruited by the British Secret Service to kill Boy B; and that once the job was done he would be rewarded with a job as well as a sexual relationship with the 39-year-old woman spy he thought he was talking to in the chatroom. The two boys later met in the flesh, and became friends, although their chatroom interaction continued, with Boy B introducing a series of other characters to reinforce Boy A's deception. Boy A was also persuaded of the fact that B was suffering from a cancerous tumour, and eventually carried out 'orders', stabbing Boy B in the chest and stomach. Boy B survived, though, and police later reconstructed the story from computer chatroom text. Detective Chief Inspector Ross said there was nothing in Boy B's background to suggest why he wanted to die. 'We have not come across any underlying things that would turn a child to do this sort of thing,' he said.

Family Life

Keep it in the family – weirdness, that is …

A Chinese woman went down an unconventional route to becoming a grandmother – she advertised in her local newspaper. Liu Lan, 64, from Chengdu, ✳ Sichuan province, has a son, but although he has been married for 11 years, he has no intention of having children. So after drawn-out arguments with her son, Liu tried another way, and put the following ad in her local paper: 'I would love to recruit a three-person family who have a little child as my relatives. After six months, if they are qualified, I would allow them to live with me. Then I can enjoy being a real granny.' At the time of writing, she had had several replies to her ad.

Australian Health Minister Tony Abbott made the news with a heartwarming story when it turned out that his long-lost son, Daniel O'Connor, was actually working in the same building as him. The minister, believing himself to be too young at the age of 19 to face the responsibility of fatherhood (and the boy's mother was even younger, at 17), had given the boy up for adoption. When Abbott finally traced the boy they were reunited to some fanfare – but it wasn't long before DNA tests were taken, and it turned out that after 27 years of waiting and wondering (and assuming)

love your mother...

Kailashgiri Brahmachari, from the northern Indian state of Madhya Pradesh, has been on a mother-venerating pilgrimage for several years now. Kailashgiri has been carrying his mother around India in a basket suspended from a bar that sits on his shoulders. Kailashgiri's mother, Kethakdevi, who is blind, said once that she would like to visit all of India's holy sites, and in honour of his mother's wish, her son felt obliged to help her achieve her goal. He carries his mother in one basket and their few earthly possessions in another, and he manages to walk about 10 km a day. They expect to be on the road until 2013. Kailashgiri is now revered as a wise man, but his mother says she's getting a bit tired of it all and wishes sometimes she was back home.

then the tearful reunion, O'Connor was not his son after all – his mother had not been quite truthful about things all those years ago.

HATE YOUR MOTHER ...

A Brazilian man visited his 88-year-old mother in São Paolo to steal her pension to buy drink with. When she expressed her reluctance to hand her money over to Luiz Polidoro, 48, he picked her up and dumped her over the fence into next door's yard, where the neighbour's two pit bull terriers mauled her to death.

It doesn't get much more gruesome and grisly than this, so be warned ... In Amsterdam a man was arrested one night wearing the most macabre of outfits – his own mother's skin. The 42-year-old man had apparently murdered his 76-year-old mother (he bludgeoned her to death), skinned and then gone walkabout in the city centre wearing the fatty, bloody skin draped over his shoulders. Passers-by assumed he was wearing a carnival fancy dress outfit, until he was arrested and taken to a police station where the hideous truth came to light.

... AND HATE YOUR WIFE

Because his wife had not succeeded in bearing any children for him, a Bengali man buried his

25-year-old wife alive in a large pit. Three days later she was rescued – still alive – when heavy rains washed away soil covering the pit. That won't get her pregnant, will it?

... AND HATE YOUR BROTHER

In the US state of Minnesota, Jose Juarez, 45, insulted the daughter of his younger brother, Roy, and a fight ensued. At its peak, Jose grabbed brother Roy's right hand and bit off the top part of his middle finger. Roy was taken to hospital, where the finger part was re-attached to the hand, while Jose ended up in court charged with assault.

An Israeli businessman was on a work trip to the Red Sea resort of Eilat. At the end of the first day he did the businessman-away-from-his-wife thing and arranged for a prostitute to be sent up to his hotel room to relieve his executive stress. Just imagine the poor man's surprise when he instantly recognised the young woman who walked into his room as his very own daughter. The father cut short his stay in Eilat and on his return home recounted his story to his wife, who, distraught, vowed both to find her daughter and help her find a better life, and divorce her scumbag husband.

A Saudi woman in her fifties succeeded last year in getting her hands on her inheritance – but she had to have surgery first. The woman had hidden nine gold rings, three chains, three charms and three bags of money in her womb to stop her thieving brothers getting their hands on it all. They had locked her in a room for 11 years after she threatened to tell police that they had stolen her share of inheritances from their father and her deceased husband.

... and your son

A father and son row over a recipe for cooking chicken ended in an excess of violence. The pair began arguing about how best to cook the chicken for their dinner and ended up firing .22 calibre handguns at each other at their home in the US state of West Virginia. The father, Jackie Lee Shrader, 49, ended up shooting his son, Harley Lee, in the head and was charged with malicious wounding and wanton endangerment. And after being treated in hospital, Harley Shrader was also charged with wanton endangerment.

PARENTING

His leg was broken, her waters had broken ... In an interesting and innovative approach to being present at the birth of his child, Trent Ashton watched his son being born from a hospital bed after breaking his leg the same day the baby started to arrive. While Mr Ashton suffered his severe injury playing rugby 30 miles from home, his wife Rachel called to say her waters had broken. Ashton asked if he could be taken to the same hospital where his wife was in labour, then further made a nuisance of himself by refusing surgery on his leg until he was taken to the maternity ward. Eventually he was put in a bed next to his wife and watched as his son Jack Joseph was delivered by Caesarean.

Here's a sorry irony. A British woman who had decided not to have any more children for herself, but who went through a surrogate pregnancy for another couple, died giving birth to the baby. The pregnancy had not been at all problematic, and she gave birth to a healthy 11 lb baby, but two hours after the delivery she had a heart attack and died. The client couple was given the baby a few weeks afterwards.

First the sad bit: in California, John Dunton's infant daughter died when he left her in his minivan, having forgotten to drop her off at their babysitter's on his way to work. Then the weird bit: when Dunton was informed that no criminal charges would be filed, he appeared at a press conference and boasted that a jury would have acquitted him anyway; then made a statement imploring car manufacturers to invent something to keep parents from forgetting about their kids.

As punishment for their naughty behaviour, a Californian father decided that his children wouldn't be getting their Christmas presents, three Nintendo games systems. To really rub it in, he put them up for sale on an Internet auction site, and cleaned up to the tune of $5300. And if that wasn't bad enough, the kids had to sit and watch as the money gained from their games was donated to a local church.

There is a year in their lives that many American parents regard with a mixture of anxiety and relief: the year their child goes to college. For a couple from the US state of Maryland the son in question is a Cabbage Patch doll, which is kind of weird. Joe and Pat Posey have for the last 19 years raised 'Kevin', as they christened the doll, as their own son (they have a grown-up daughter, Vicky, but they prefer Kevin). Kevin goes everywhere with them, joining in with their conversations (Joe does Kevin's voice), playing in his own 100 square foot room in the couple's house, joining his dad on fishing trips and revelling in the £2000 fund the couple have put aside for college. Kevin should do well at college, since, as father Joe says, 'He makes friends easily.'

KIDS

What's a nice way of having a memento of your newborn? Most people go for boring old photos and a bit of video footage. Well, South Korean parents can now preserve their child's umbilical cord in acrylic resin, or even have it gold-plated. U&I Impression has gold-plated up to 100 umbilical cords a month since starting business last year, with prices ranging from £40 to £50.

This kid must either love school with a burning passion, or be totally terrified of the consequences of missing a day. Either way, this story is a little weird. An eight-year-old German boy was found by police patrolmen in the city of Aachen at 3 am after he had woken up in the middle of the night, picked up his school stuff and hurried out, anxious to get on with his education. When he found the school very closed indeed, he turned round and headed home. He told officers that when he had woken up he had misread the time on his alarm clock and thought he was late for school. The officers delivered the boy back to his parents, who were still asleep, unaware of their son's little excursion.

WEIRD

With his mother completely unaware that he was even up and awake, let alone getting up to some serious mischief, a four-year-old boy took her car to a video store in the middle of the night and back. He was too little to reach the accelerator pedal, but he managed to put the car into gear and steer it as it moved forward. When he got to the video store, not far from his home in the US state of Michigan, the boy was disappointed to find it was closed – it was 1.30 am, after all – and so he began the journey home. A police officer saw the car, no lights on, weaving all over the road, travelling at about 5 mph, and followed it into the car park of an apartment block and watched as it hit two parked cars. The officer put on his car's flashing blue light and the boy immediately put his mum's car in reverse and drove into the police car. No charges were filed against the four-year-old.

TEENS

Seventeen-year-old Christian Silbereis got into a bit of trouble for his choice of costume for his school's Halloween fancy dress day. Silbereis went to his school, in Ann Arbor, in the US state of Michigan, dressed as a vagina. Although his classmates at Community High School were not particularly offended by the outfit, which was made by Silbereis's mother from a pink cape, the school administrators suspended him for the rest of the week. Silbereis's costume was 'anatomically correct' – his mother is a midwife and had used the outfit before at a midwife's party – and won first prize in the school's costume contest. And he was a little perplexed by his punishment: 'It's just another body part,' he said. 'They teach us about it in school.'

Education

We spend all this money and time on educating people, and what happens?

Discipline may be a byword in Japanese institutions but even by their standards this example is a bit beyond the pale. At a school in Fukuoka a teacher caught one of his pupils, a 17-year-old boy, snoozing in class and told him to report to the staff room, where he exacted a very extreme punishment on the lad. He handed the boy a box-cutter and told him to write an apology for falling asleep in class – in his own blood – then left him to carry out the order. The boy dutifully cut his finger with the box-cutter and used his blood as ink for the apology, without any of the other teachers in the staff room apparently noticing what was going on. The teacher eventually apologised to his head and to the boy and his family, but neither the boy or his parents asked for the teacher to be removed.

There was a teensy-weensy problem, darlings, at a private college in Chiang Mai, Thailand: some of girls started complaining that their toilets were being invaded by the college's transvestites and transsexuals. It seems that there are about 15 young men at the college who have difficulties with their gender, and that most of the other young men were having difficulties with their gender too, hence a steady stream of teasing and bullying. So the college designated a 'pink lotus' toilet exclusively for their use. Problem solved – no more complaints from the girls that they were hogging the mirrors, and an improvement in academic results from the 15 boys, happy with their own 'third sex' toilet.

A primary school in Austria has been testing a cruel device that unfairly stops children from dropping off in class. Purpose-built wobbly chairs, inflicted on pupils at Thaur primary school, allegedly help children to concentrate better by keeping them awake. The

A school in Nottingham is facing up to the grim reality of children smoking and has been offering free nicotine patches to fag-ash kids to help them stub out the habit. Sixteen pupils at the William Sharp comprehensive were enrolled in anti-smoking sessions, with seven of them successfully kicking the habit thanks to the patches.

chairs were made by sadistic teacher Andreas Prochaska, who said he got the design from a musician friend of his.

It appears that a prank to sabotage lessons in Romanian schools caught on in a big way last year. Kids were using the processed cheese that they get in sandwiches, given to them as break-time snacks, to smear onto the blackboards, creating a greasy layer that stops chalk working and requiring the blackboard to be thoroughly washed down with detergent. The idea started in the town of Iasi, where the local authority spokesperson admitted that the situation was 'serious', and that the practice was spreading. Officials were planning to give the students milk instead of cheese in the future.

At morning assembly in a Manchester school one day last year, a teacher told 230 14-year-old pupils that an asteroid was on collision course with Earth, that it was to strike very shortly, and that they could all go home early to say their final farewells to their families. The idea of the spoof announcement was to kick off the theme of the assembly, that of 'seizing the day' and making the most of every moment of life, but many of the kids panicked, broke down in tears immediately and the head of year had to be called in to calm things down.

Accident & Injury

QUIRKY
BIZARRE
ODD

When a neighbour saw something very gruesome indeed in John Hutcherson's truck one morning, Hutcherson, 21, was arrested at his home in Marietta, in the US state of Georgia. It seems that there was a headless body in there, something which Hutcherson claimed he knew nothing about – but since it was a good friend, this could hardly be true. The two had been driving in the truck the night before when Hutcherson, drunk, veered off the road, and the friend, with his head out of the window to see what was going on, was decapitated by a telegraph pole guide wire. Hutcherson just drove home and went to bed, with his pal's corpse still slumped over the truck door.

Keith Caldwell was probably hopping mad after he shot himself by mistake. Caldwell, of the US state of Alabama, has only one leg, and when he heard a noise in the night, grabbed his gun and got up to investigate, he didn't bother fitting his false leg. As he hopped around the house, probably rather sleepily, he lost his balance and his gun went off.

In a silly little catalogue of errors, the gun of an off-duty policeman was fired twice accidentally, hitting another man. Officer Craig Clancy, in the US city of San Antonio, was in a cubicle in a public toilet answering a call of nature. As he pulled down his trousers, his gun started to slip out of its holster. Clancy grabbed for it, his finger got stuck on the trigger, and the gun fired off two quick shots. A bullet went through the wall of the cubicle and hit the leg of a man who was happily washing his hands, with no plans to go from the toilet to hospital, which is where in fact he ended up.

FRYING PAN TO FIRE ...

A Bulgarian hunter freed himself from the clutches of a bear, saving his own life in the process, then accidentally shot himself in the head. Marin Cogev was attacked from behind by a 700 lb bear, which wrapped its forelegs around him and started to claw him. Cogev whacked the beast on the head with his rifle butt and then fired a shot into the air, causing the bear to run away. Cogev turned to pursue the bear and tripped over the rifle, which fired a bullet that creased his forehead, knocking him out. A fellow hunter found him after the attack, and later he received treatment for a punctured lung and broken ribs inflicted by the bear.

revenge of the blazing bunny

When groundsmen at the Devizes Cricket Club in Wiltshire lit a bonfire that they had first doused with paraffin, a rabbit sprinted out of it, its little cottontail alight, and ran away from view. The men soon found out where it had gone when their equipment shed suddenly went up in flames, causing £60,000 worth of damage.

Two young New Zealanders were involved in a high-speed car crash near the town of Taupo, when the one who was driving lost control on a bend and skidded into the pole supporting 11,000-volt power lines. Amazingly, they stepped out of the car completely unharmed – and that's when they suffered serious injuries. It was raining, and they both stood in a pool of rainwater electrified by the power lines. Both men suffered electric shocks and one was badly burned.

A 23-year-old woman from Sale, Cheshire, tried to alleviate the tedium of sitting with her fingers in solution to remove her false nails by lighting a scented candle. Surprise, surprise, the highly flammable acetone caught fire. The woman then very sensibly picked up the flaming bowl and ran around the house with it, splashing burning liquid onto the carpet and two settees, all of which burst into flames too. She tried to beat out the flames, but, would you believe it, her hands caught fire too. Trying a different tack, the woman ran into her kitchen and threw the bowl away from her, which would have been a good plan had she not thrown it in such a way as to set the cooker's electrics on fire. Eventually the fire brigade arrived to put matters right.

A 33-year-old Welsh housewife ended up in hospital after fainting in her local Asda supermarket, collapsing and knocking her head against a shelf. Her fainting fit was brought on by wearing a pair of vibrating 'passion pants' bought in an erotic lingerie store (not Asda). The vibrating bullet inside the pants so aroused her, apparently, that she completely passed out and whacked her head. Paramedics found her unconscious with a faint buzzing noise emanating from her front bottom. They expertly deactivated the unusual underwear, took her to hospital, where she recovered, and discharged her with her the passion pants discreetly packed in a bag.

A driver in Essex suffered a straightforward injury – a broken nose – from a very unusual cause: a frozen sausage. The man was driving with his window down near his home in South Woodham Ferrers, in Essex, when a car passed in the other direction, the sausage flew through his window and he felt a sudden sharp pain in his nose. He managed to slow down and stop safely and discovered his nose was broken. Police were investigating to find the identity of the phantom frozen-sausage-thrower.

A 21-year-old Australian man ended up in intensive care after his bar-room drinking trick didn't have the desired effect. The man ran a hose from a beer pump into a beer jug, and connected the beer jug to a helmet he was wearing. The pump was powered by an electric drill, and the idea was to give himself a steady

stuck!

A Slovak man was driving in the Tatra Mountains, on a winter holiday, when an avalanche struck, completely covering his car. Richard Kral opened the car window to dig his way out, but quickly realised that there was so much snow that it would force its way into the car well before he could get out to safety. Kral opened a bottle of beer while he had a good think about his predicament, and soon realised that he had the answer in his hand. Kral had stocked up for his holiday well, packing 60 half-litre bottles of beer, and he saw that he could melt the snow that was above the car by urinating on it. Kral set to work scooping snow down to below the level of the window and, steadfastly working his way through the beer, urinating on it to melt it. Four days and 30 litres of beer later, Kral was found by a rescue team, staggering along a mountain path, completely drunk, suffering from very sore kidneys and with an unusual tale to tell.

flow of beer without having to lift up a glass and swallow. However, the flow from the drill-powered pump was far too strong, and he was rushed to hospital with a 10 cm tear in his stomach.

A teenager in Macedonia could never in a million years have guessed what he had found and tried to cut up for scrap metal, but the strange-looking object very nearly killed him. Milan Petrov, 16, from the town of Vinica, found a cloud-seeding missile in a forest near his house and brought it home to cut up for scrap. But when he attacked it with a heavy axe in order to break it up, the missile, used to influence rain-bearing clouds, exploded, injuring him badly. Now he'll know what a cloud-seeding missile is if he ever sees one again.

Palo Verde nuclear generating station, in Arizona, is the biggest nuclear electric plant in the US, but something as insignificant as a bit of bird poo caused wide-ranging blackouts. It is thought that a splat of bird dropping short-circuited a unit at the power plant and there were power cuts as a result across Arizona, New Mexico, California and even as far north as Alberta in Canada.

Was it the Hand of God? Or a message from the Mob? New York police were bemused when they

Someone could have created the biggest omelette in the world last year in Texas, when a truck carrying 13,500 kg of eggs spilled its load off a flyover. The motorway below had to be shut down and the stench was truly overpowering as clean-up workers struggled to stay on their feet amid the slippery mess. It took over 14 hours, with the eggs slowly congealing and going off in the sun, to get rid of the spillage.

received a call from a boat owner who was out on the water near Long Island, heard the thump of an object landing on the deck of his boat and found a human hand. Police searches for the hand's owner have so far proved fruitless, and the mystery was still unsolved at the time of writing.

She meant well, of course, but the Peruvian school teacher who used a traditional shampoo to get rid of head lice on some of her pupils got it badly wrong when the mixture ran into their eyes and blinded them. The shampoo, a mixture of alcohol and the seeds of a fruit called the cherimoya, appeared to have damaged the retinas of four of her pupils and left 20 suffering from severe eye irritation. Doctors were still trying to determine whether the blindness was permanent.

DRUNKENNESS

That's it, bypass that clumsy, old-fashioned, slow way of drinking beer using a boring old glass ... A Czech man in the town of Brno hid in the toilet of a restaurant until all the staff had left, broke the door behind which the beer kegs were kept and hooked the pipes up directly to his mouth. Cleaning staff later found him on the floor of the restaurant bar, completely drunk and incapable. He was later prosecuted for the damage he caused.

Any excuse ... fishermen in western Russia said last year that they were driven to drink by a UFO that regularly passes over them. In a location near the city of Yekaterinburg, locals claim to have seen on many occasions a small green UFO during the last two years, most recently sighted in June 2005. And the consensus was that seeing the UFO made them feel anxious. But the local fishermen went one step further, saying that every time it passes over them it leaves them with an almost unquenchable thirst for alcohol.

Out on a little island just off the coast of New York state, Thomas Woods and Rod Bennett were at the house of Mr Woods having a little drink or two. Woods decided to make an alcohol-fuelled dare to his friend, setting fire to the rug and challenging the pair of them to see who could stay in the house the longest. Bennett fled to call the fire brigade when flames started to engulf the house, making Woods the winner – even though he was in a way the loser too, since he didn't make it out of the house alive. And the name of that little island? Fire Island.

Ah, the thrill of the enema – that bubbling feeling in your nether regions. So I've been told. And how much better if there's booze in it too. A Texas woman was indicted for criminally negligent homicide for causing her husband's death by giving him a sherry enema. And it wasn't a little snifter that she was accused of having passed up his backside, oh no: Tammy Jean Warner, 42, gave Michael Warner two 1.5 litre bottles of sherry. His blood alcohol level shot up to 0.47 per cent, or nearly six times the level considered legally drunk in Texas. Warner, 58, supposedly had a throat problem that meant he was unable to drink the sherry. Warner had been addicted to enemas since childhood, and had a collection of enema 'recipes' that he regularly enjoyed.

THINGS INSIDE YOU THAT REALLY SHOULDN'T BE THERE

A Chinese man aged 24 went into hospital in the city of Hengyang with head pains, and it was decided that an operation was necessary. Surgeons opened up his skull to find there was a five-inch worm living in his brain. The sparganum worm, a species of tapeworm, probably arrived in the man's body after he ate wild snake or frog, both of which carry the parasite, and made its way up to the brain once it was established inside the body.

When a Hong Kong woman on a hiking trip washed her face in a freshwater stream, she didn't notice anything out of the ordinary. About two weeks later her nose started bleeding, and basically carried on bleeding intermittently. The first doctor the woman visited found nothing when he examined her, but the second doctor was more successful. He discovered a leech hiding in her left nostril, sticking stubbornly to the inside and living off her blood. A quick tug with a pair of forceps, after a shot of anaesthetic, and the leech was removed from her nose.

An 84-year-old Thai man was suffering from a persistent itching in his ears, and had scratched them so much with cotton buds that they started bleeding, so he went to hospital. Doctors found around 50 maggots in his ears, and removed them one by one with tweezers and a special suction device. They kept him in to see if any more hatched from the fly eggs that had probably been laid inside his ears.

When Sherry Fuller, 31, returned to her home in Essex after a spell of voluntary work in Madagascar, she became unable to speak clearly, and, worse, her limbs began to twitch without her being able to control them. Finally she collapsed, and was rushed to hospital, where doctors discovered a nest of larvae happily growing inside her brain. The pressure on her brain was causing the symptoms, and after being zapped with drugs the little maggotty creatures were killed off. Fuller was given a check-up just in case anything else had taken up residence and a six-inch-long worm was found to be living in her intestine.

MAKING A MESS OF YOUR GENITALS ...

What planet you live on when you can 'accidentally' cut off your penis and 'accidentally' feed it to your dog is anyone's guess. The potential otherworldly being in question is 67-year-old Constantin Mocanu, a Romanian who told doctors that a noisy chicken was stopping him from getting his beauty sleep, so he went out with the intention of chopping its raucous head off. Mocanu claimed that he mistook his penis for the chicken's neck (both scrawny and wrinkly – a mistake anyone could make, and the bird in question was in fact a cock) and had at it with his chopper. He was so cross with himself

A Welsh rugby fan told fellow drinkers at his social club in Caerphilly, south Wales, that if Wales beat England in the upcoming Six Nations international he would cut his balls off. And with Wales not having beaten England for 12 years, it looked as though he would not have to honour his promise. But when Wales sneaked an 11–9 win, Geoff Huish, 26, went home, took a knife and did the deed, walking the short distance back to the social club to brandish his testicles and show his astounded mates what he had done. **ECCENTRIC** when he realised what he had done that he threw the severed organ to the dog before his wife called for an ambulance. Mocanu was rushed to hospital where his life, but not his penis, was saved by a surgeon who viewed the man's story with some scepticism.

A burglar broke into the house of pensioners Joyce and Leslie Edwards in Crowthorne, Berkshire, and suffered a horrendous mishap on the way in. Mrs Edwards heard the sound of breaking glass in her bathroom during the night, and when the 80-year-old went to see what was happening, she found a man half in

When you're bursting for a pee and someone says 'Tie a knot in it', it's not to be taken seriously. But a Romanian man did something very similar and suffered very nasty consequences. Vasile Barbulescu tied string around his penis in order to avoid having to urinate until he got home from a journey. He ended up in hospital, having bound up his penis very tightly indeed, and suffered massive injuries to the organ. Doctors were unsure whether the damage could be undone, even after extensive surgery.

and half out of the window with a long shard of glass stuck firmly into his genitals – it had sliced off one of his testicles. Blood had started to gush copiously from the wound, and the thief pleaded for help. Mrs Edwards was too shaken to call the police, but went to her neighbours who alerted the emergency services. By the time they arrived, the man had been impaled by his genitals on the glass spike for about an hour, and had lost about four pints of blood. Which was no more than he deserved, according to his potential victim.

... AND OF OTHER PEOPLE'S

Romanian surgeon Naum Ciomu was operating on a 34-year-old man with a testicular problem when he accidentally sliced through the man's urinary channel with his scalpel. In a petulant fit of rage (never a useful emotion as a surgeon) Ciomu slashed the man's penis into three pieces. The patient was rushed to another hospital for emergency surgery in which a new penis was constructed from skin from the man's forearm, while Dr Ciomu was barred from surgery for six months while he was investigated by a medical council.

Amanda Monti took revenge for being rejected by ripping off her ex-boyfriend's testicle with her bare hands. The Merseyside couple, Monti, 24, and Geoffrey Jones, 37, had split up a few weeks earlier, when Jones ended their relationship. They met up at a barbecue, apparently on good terms, and Monti offered to drive him back to his house, where an impromptu party started, as friends arrived and drink started flowing. Towards the end of the party, Monti found Jones and offered him sex. He refused. She got very angry, and attacked him, ending up on the floor at his feet, from which position she reached up, gripped his genitals and pulled hard. Very hard. So hard that a testicle popped out. Jones, in agony, didn't realise the extent of the damage, and Monti at first tried to hide the testicle in her mouth. She eventually put it in the hands of a friend, who walked over to Jones and informed him that this was his testicle. Later, in hospital, doctors were unable to reattach it.

Up there in the wildest state of the US, things do occasionally get ... wild. In the city of Anchorage, a 44-year-old man and his girlfriend were in the throes of breaking up one night, but somewhere in the arguments, accusations and recriminations they decided to have sex; and indeed, sex involving the man having his arms tied up by his soon-to-be ex-girlfriend. Instead of proceeding with the sex thing, she took a kitchen knife, cut off his penis and flushed it down the toilet. She then kindly untied him, drove him to hospital, then went back to clean up all the bloodstains, which was where the police found her. The officers arrested her, and also called in workers from the water company, who dismantled the toilet and removed it, enabling them to retrieve the severed penis and deliver it to the hospital, where surgeons successfully reattached it.

DSO (DICK SHOT OFF)

Gang member Robert Johnson in the US state of North Carolina punished a fellow Blood who wanted to quit the gang by shooting him in the leg. Unfortunately for the victim the bullet went right through his leg and took off his penis. Johnson got 15 years in jail for

More grim crims shooting each other in painful places, this time in Newcastle: a court heard how a hitman, Arthur Pattinson, was hired to kill Stanley Cresswell. The man who took out the £60,000 contract, Thomas Anderson, turned up at the scene of the hit to point Cresswell out to Pattinson so that he could then shoot him. Cresswell spotted Anderson and walked up to him just as Pattinson decided to shoot. The bullet went through Cresswell's arm – not killing him at all – and was deflected into Anderson's genitals, making a right mess of them. Kind of serves him right.

'non-malicious castration' – that is, he intended to shoot his victim, but not to shoot off his genitals.

PROBLEMS WITH POINTY THINGS

Hospital staff in the Polish town of Wojnowice were treating a retired school teacher for a headache when they found a five-inch knife blade lodged in his head. Sixty-one-year-old Leonard Woronowicz had hit his head when he tripped over in his kitchen a few days earlier – the floor was scattered with various DIY tools – and there was a small gash near his ear. Woronowicz put a plaster on it and carried on with his life, but the ache from the wound got worse, so he decided to see

When drugs police raided Mao Qiang's flat in the Chinese city of Chengdu he wanted to avoid being caught for illegal possession of a dangerous weapon. So he took prompt action and swallowed his three-inch knife. Later, he couldn't get it out, and there the folding knife stayed, lodged firmly in his trachea for eight long and very uncomfortable months before he finally sought medical assistance. The surgeons who removed the knife told him that it could have caused his death at any moment. **STUPID** a doctor. The X-ray showed a five-inch blade, which had snapped off from the handle as his head landed on it, inside his skull. The blade had not touched any major blood vessels or nerves, or even caused any serious damage. This also was the solution to the mystery of where his kitchen knife had disappeared to.

A dentist found the cause of the toothache Patrick Lawler, resident of the US state of Colorado, was complaining about: a 10 cm nail. Lawler, a building worker, had unwittingly embedded the nail in his skull six days earlier when a nail gun backfired on him. The tool sent a nail into a piece of wood nearby, but Lawler didn't realise that a second nail had shot through his mouth. After painkillers and ice didn't ease the pain, he saw a dentist, who broke the news to him, then was taken to a Denver hospital where four hours of surgery were needed to remove the nail, which had just missed his right eye.

Steve Villagomez, a 29-year-old football coach in California, thought he had injured his neck during a football practice last year, and went to see a doctor, who carried out an X-ray. The X-ray revealed what appeared to be a metal object in his neck, but Villagomez just couldn't see how the diagnosis could be correct and ignored it. A couple of months later, Villagomez told some of his fellow coaches about the bizarre X-ray, and one of them jokingly suggested putting a magnet to his neck. Villagomez took his advice and began experiencing pain in his jaw and neck, so he visited another doctor, who confirmed the original diagnosis and convinced him it would be a good idea to have an operation. The doctor extracted a two-inch-long rusty nail from Villagomez's neck, and although the nail could have been buried in his neck anywhere from six months to several years, Villagomez had never experienced pain from it, other than during that one football practice, and had absolutely no idea how the nail had got there in the first place.

A Russian man had a heavy drinking session with a friend, went to bed and woke up with a splitting headache. Nothing too odd about that. Except in this case, there was something nightmarishly odd about it. Artur Dzhavanyan had invited a mate round for a drink, but as the evening went on, he told his friend that he was sick of listening to him complaining all the time, and lurched off to bed, immediately falling into a drunken sleep. He woke up after a while with the usual hamster-cage mouth, and went into his bathroom for a glass of water, and saw in the bathroom mirror his own face with a kitchen knife sticking into it. That would explain the really bad headache. Dzhavanyan ran to a neighbour's house and called an ambulance, was rushed to hospital and had the knife removed with minimal damage to his

serves you right

Jerry Allen Bradford of Pensacola, Florida, was shot during a puppy-killing spree by one of the puppies. Bradford had a litter of three-month-old pups he claimed he couldn't get rid of, and was saving himself the cost of puppy food by shooting them one by one. He had already killed three when he got a taste of his own medicine: the next puppy to get the bullet started to wriggle free, its paw hit the trigger of the gun, and Bradford was shot in the wrist. A doctor who treated him also told the authorities, and Bradford went on a felony charge for animal cruelty.

facial nerves. His friend's fingerprints were on the knife, but Dzhavanyan refused to press charges, saying he was just happy to be alive.

Human Error

To err is human. To note it down is my job.

The residents of a village in eastern Romania panicked and fled when they believed that the village was about to be invaded by aliens. The people of Cristinesti saw coloured lights in the sky one night and word quickly spread that UFOs were attacking the region, causing a mass desertion of the village. Police, called out to investigate, soon worked out that the lights were from an open-air disco a few miles away and managed to persuade the villagers that there was no extraterrestrial attack being carried out. One villager went on record as saying how pleased he was that they had escaped an alien invasion.

In Aracruz, a sleepy little town in Brazil, residents were terrified when a fireball fell from the sky, and even more in fear of their lives when a small, badly burned creature, clearly an alien, was found. Over 50 people called the police station to say that an alien invasion was taking place, and the body was taken to the local hospital where doctors were able to call on all their expertise to identify the body as that of a burned rubber doll.

A Chinese woman was taken to hospital after being attacked by a tiger – as she believed. The woman passed by a dark alleyway in the city of Shanghai and saw a tiger hiding there, ready to pounce. She turned and fled, slipped on some ice and fell heavily, injuring herself, and had to be taken to hospital. The tiger was a painting hung in the window of a shop and backlit for a lifelike effect; so lifelike that when passers-by came to the woman's help she was still repeating, 'There's a tiger, a tiger,' and pointing in terror down the alley.

Ukrainian firemen were attending a fire at a health club in the city of Donetsk. One firefighter tripped over what he thought was a loose hosepipe, and picked it up, planning to use it on the blaze. When he realised it was a 10-foot python and not a hosepipe at all he fled in panic, with his colleagues soon joining him. The men were eventually talked into going back to fight the fire by the owner of the building, who said the python, an office pet, was harmless. They put out the fire and even pulled the python out to safety by its tail.

An elderly woman called the RSPCA, they reported, to inform them that she had been looking after an abandoned hedgehog and would they please collect it. When officers arrived they found it was a conker shell.

A doctor was called to the deathbed of an 87-year-old man in Latvia's capital city Riga. The doctor noted the cause of death as 'old age' and went on his way – completely failing to take into account the fact that there were no less then 45 stab wounds on the body. It was only when mortuary workers began to prepare the body for cremation that the doctor's howler was revealed. A murder inquiry was launched, rather later than it should have been.

The government of Sudan had a nasty surprise when it read what the United States Congress website had to say about some nuclear testing it had just done. According to the site, nuclear tests had been carried out in Sudan between 1962 and 1970.

forgetfulness

Sometimes it takes a while for the penny to drop. A Malaysian couple, Tu Fu Qiang and Lai Chai Zhen, got married back in 1989. When, 15 years later, one of the kids asked to see the wedding photos, they suddenly realised they had forgotten to pick them up from the photographer's. Tu Fu and Lai Chai decided to see if their photos, on which they had paid a £7 deposit, might still be there. Amazingly, they were still waiting to be collected and the studio owner let them have the snaps half-price.

When the agitated Sudanese Foreign Minister Mustafa Osman Ismail raised it with US officials in Khartoum, it turned out that there had been a typing error. The report should have said Sedan, a test site in the US state of Nevada.

There was more than a little dismay in Norway as TV viewers observed the inauguration of US President George W. Bush – he made a hand gesture that seemed to demonstrate that he was in league with the Devil. The president and family were shown lifting their right hands with their index and little fingers extended, which in Norway would be seen as a salute to the Devil. 'Shock greeting from Bush daughter', read a headline in the Norwegian Internet newspaper *Nettavisen*, above a photograph of Bush's daughter, Jenna, smiling and apparently saluting Satan. In reality, it was a sign of support for the University of Texas Longhorns. Bush, a former Texas governor, was simply greeting the Texas Longhorn marching band as it passed during the parade in the president's honour.

Plain Stupid

DUMB, DUMBER AND DUMBEST ...

Nice try, but no cigar ... Frances Lea Shaw, 41, of the US state of Pennsylvania set her house on fire for the insurance, and then called firefighters. Why didn't her cunning plan succeed? Police and firefighters very quickly noticed that Shaw had stashed all her valuable stuff, like the TV, good clothes, microwave, under a tarpaulin away from the blaze. She was charged with arson.

The stupidity of some people knows no bounds, apparently, at least not in the US state of Florida. After screaming out to her friends, 'See what I can still do,' a 23-year-old woman plunged to her death attempting to do a handstand on the railing of a hotel balcony.

So these two guys in the US state of Idaho were having fun shooting at a protective vest outdoors. It wasn't designed to stop bullets, only grenade fragments, but it looked like it worked, so one of them, Alexander Swandic, put it on and told his buddy, David Hueth, to go ahead and shoot him right in the chest. And guess what? Hueth fired, and Swandic died of a gunshot wound to the heart.

A Belgian man in the town of Schaarbeek suffered the loss of his pet dog, and the grief obviously rendered him extremely stupid. He attempted to carry out a home cremation, using his barbecue, and with the apartment terrace as the venue. He sloshed far too much petrol onto the barbecue, and the wall of flames that shot up set the building alight. The fire brigade put the fire out, and the owner had to go to hospital for treatment – but we don't know if the dog was fully cremated or not.

In New York City, teacher Wayne Brightly was finding it difficult to pass the state's modest certi-fication exam, so he paid a former mentor, Rubin Leitner, to take the test for him. Mr Brightly is 38, black, and rather thin, so it will surprise you to learn that the man he stupidly selected to represent him and potentially be questioned on the exam was 58, white, plump and suffering from Asperger's syndrome. Although Leitner used fake ID, his super scores in the exam were so far removed from what Brightly had managed in earlier exams that officials requested a meeting with Brightly. And even more stupidly, Brightly actually sent Leitner along to the meeting. End of attempted deception.

VICTIMS TOO STUPID TO DESERVE OUR SYMPATHY

A Japanese woman took a telephone call from someone claiming to be her son, asking for money to pay off a loan. The man, whom the woman believed was her son, asked her to deposit a sum of nearly £6000 into a particular bank account, and she was only to happy to oblige. The rather silly thing about this is that her son was in the house, in bed, at the time of the call.

 An Irish man, whose name has not been revealed for obvious reasons of deep embarrassment, was

A Zimbabwean woman lost a lot of money when she paid for help in recovering her stolen car. Magrate Mapfumo paid Edna Chizema about £2800 to fly four invisible mermaids from London to assist in the recovery of her car. Yes, that's four invisible mermaids, those well-known car-finders from a city renowned for its supply of high-quality invisible mermaids. Well worth the money. **QUIRKY**

approached in the town of Kilkenny and offered the once-in-a-lifetime chance of buying a brand new state-of-the-art laptop for a mere €700 (about £500). Now we know that buying a computer from a man in the street is possibly one of the surest ways to lose a lot of money, so we can only praise our hero for his refreshing naivety and optimism (and ignore the enormous idiocy). He gave the computer vendor the money in cash there and then and was given a laptop carrying case with, apparently, a laptop in side – but the buyer didn't even open the case until later, when he found that he had been sold a lovely laptop case with four litres of milk inside. And with a flash of profound wisdom, Sgt Pat Murphy of Kilkenny Garda Station later said people should only buy computers from legitimate vendors.

An 81-year-old German man responded to a request from two young women to join in a naked photo shoot. Believing that they really wanted him and his wrinkly parts in a photo, the old codger swiftly got his kit off, whereupon the girls nicked everything, including his wallet with about £150 in it.

A (male) gynaecologist who offers free examinations? And who runs his practice out of a self-storage locker? You'd smell a rat wouldn't you? But no, apparently there was a steady stream of female customers in Dallas, Texas, unable to smell rats and too stupid to realise that despite all the above Thomas Remo, 50, was not in fact a real gynaecologist. Remo was eventually arrested last year.

In Florida, Aravis Walker, 23, had a great game he would play, in which he would drive around lighting fireworks and throw them out of his car window at innocent pedestrians. His dastardly scheme backfired on him one day when one of the fireworks bounced back inside his car and ended up in the back seat, where it ignited Walker's stash of fireworks, causing the car to explode and killing him.

A 19-year-old man in the US state of Michigan had a great plan to exercise a bit of neighbourly revenge. His ploy was to stab himself in the chest, call an ambulance and then say the neighbour, with whom he had a feud, had done it. Part I went very well – he stabbed himself in the chest. Part II went very badly – he bled to death.

ABUSING THE EMERGENCY SERVICES

German police in Cologne were called by a driver who reported that one of her two daughters had accidentally thrown her cuddly toy tiger out onto the motorway, and that it was too dangerous to try and retrieve it. She asked the police if they would be kind enough to find it. After some dispute a patrol car was eventually sent out and the toy was retrieved and returned to the little girl. Good to see that they had a firm grip on their priorities – or maybe it was just a very quiet day that day.

The Avon and Somerset police are always ready to give examples of how their emergency services are abused, in the hope of preventing further abuse. Here are a few examples from last year: one caller rang to say that his dire emergency was not being able to get his social security payments because the office had taken his book off him. As the communications operator pointed out, 'I'm afraid that's not a police matter, sir.' Another caller rang in and started off with the fatal 'I know this is going to sound stupid' – and indeed it was, and more stupid than you could imagine, since he continued to say that a pigeon had been run over ... and he had no money to phone the RSPCA. The communications operator very understandably became slightly exasperated with a caller who was phoning the life-and-death emergency line about a pigeon in the street.

In California, 44-year-old Leonardo Leyva dialled 911 (the equivalent of 999) in the small hours of the morning after rolling home drunk. He complained to the emergency services that his wife wouldn't have sex with him. Leyva was arrested shortly afterwards.

WASTING POLICE TIME

A German man's melodramatic approach to leaving his wife and family and running off with a younger woman ended up costing him £9000 for wasting police time and resources. Heinz Welsinger, 54, faked his death, leaving his motorbike on its side, engine still running, on the bank of the River Lippe, making it look as though he had had an accident and had plunged into the river. Police frogmen scoured the riverbed, and several days of searching eventually uncovered his motorbike helmet but no body. Unfortunately for Welsinger, his affair only lasted a month. He decided to return to his family, in the town of Paderborn, and had to admit to having staged his own death. The local emergency services said it was not fair that taxpayers should be liable for the cost of searching for him and he received a £9000 fine.

An elderly German woman alerted the police after she stumbled on evidence of a murder in her own garden. Iris Muller, 85, of Kassel, found a set of false teeth and a pair of glasses in her flowerbed and told the police of her suspicions. The police came and dug over her entire garden, and found nothing. When a neighbour found a wallet nearby, the mystery was solved – the wallet, glasses and false teeth were traced back to a man staggering home after a heavy drinking session.

'I remember falling over a garden wall,' he said, 'but could not remember which one.'

A woman living in the US state of Ohio sparked an international terrorist alert because she was angry with her husband. Kadrah Farah Ali, 42, was arrested after she tried to take revenge on her husband by telling the FBI that he was plotting to bomb the US and Saudi embassies in London. Ali was furious that her husband had married her for her US citizenship and then had gone to live in England, so she invented a story that he and four Moroccans were planning a bombing campaign. The FBI worked with the CIA and the authorities in the UK to follow up the story and locate Ali's husband, who was of course completely unaware that he had been fingered as a public enemy. When the FBI found out it was petty revenge they were none too pleased, and Mrs Ali faced a prison sentence for her stupidity.

WHOOPS!

Silly, silly mistakes …

A 78-year-old Australian woman opened her fridge, pulled out her medicated eyedrops and gave her eyes a few drops – at which point she realised that she had picked up a tube of superglue by mistake.

With her eyelids firmly stuck together and glue leaking through onto her eyeballs, a swift trip to hospital was in order. Fortunately for Terry Horder, nurses were able to use vegetable oil to remove the glue and no damage was done.

A German man in the town of Bielefeld had a long-standing grudge against a dentist: several years earlier, this dentist had allegedly pulled out the wrong

Would you believe it – another 'supergluing the eyes shut by mistake' story: a Thai Buddhist monk, Phra Khru Prapatworakhun, went to his temple's medicine cabinet in search of eyedrops. He took out a tube, squeezed a few drops onto the floor, and seeing a clear liquid come out was satisfied that he had found what he needed to soothe his itchy eyes. He put four drops of, yes, superglue, in each eye, and soon realised his mistake when his eyelids sealed shut. He made matters slightly worse by trying to solve the problem with paint thinner, but once he was safely in the hands of doctors at Angthong Hospital, near Bangkok, the correct solvent had him looking out at the world again.

teeth, then made a mess of the repair work, leaving the man in pain and also a constant state of anger and hatred. So after years of fuming and seething – and then a heavy drinking session – he drove to the dentist's surgery, waited until he came out, revved up the car and ran him over. Except he ran over the wrong dentist. Fortunately the injured dentist was not seriously hurt, but the 47-year-old man ended up on an attempted manslaughter charge.

Last year a London football club achieved promotion to the Premiership, but started off very much on the wrong foot when it emerged that their new football shirts had the club name wrongly spelt. Crystal Palace received delivery of a batch of shirts that read 'Chrystal Palace', making them look like idiots off the field as well as – possibly – on the field.

Embarrassment no. 1 – the man in Sydney, Australia, who tried to donate some clothes on Christmas Day by putting them into a charity recycling bin leaned too far in, fell head first and got stuck with his rear end in the air, for all the world to see – for the whole of Christmas Day. Embarrassment no. 2 – he was wearing a miniskirt at the time.

A Romanian, Petru Cioaba, bought both his wife and mistress a personalised gold necklace, each with their initials and a personalised message engraved on it. If he hadn't mixed them up he might still be enjoying his two-woman lifestyle to this day, but unfortunately his wife got the wrong sort of surprise, realising that he had a mistress for whom he was buying expensive gifts, and Cioaba soon got a message at his office that she was filing for divorce. Oh, and his mistress dumped him too.

A German woman in the city of Karlsruhe was lying on a couch in an acupuncture clinic with needles inserted in various parts of her anatomy when the lights went out. 'How nice,' she thought. 'They've turned the lights out to help me relax.' Then she heard the staff leaving and the front door being locked and realised the truth – they had all forgotten about her. The woman's cries for help went unanswered and eventually she was forced to go through the painful process of removing all the acupuncture needles herself before getting up and phoning the emergency services for help.

Britain's Ascension Island suffered at the hands of the Royal Mail for quite some time last year. Royal Mail's stupid gaffe was to send all mail addressed to residents of the tiny island either to Asuncion, capital of Paraguay, or Georgetown, Guyana, which bears the same name as Acension Island's capital. Ascension Island lies in the South Atlantic, and has a population of

A bizarrely ignorant insurance company told a Welsh customer that he would not be allowed to renew his policy – because the country he lived in did not exist. A letter from Sentinel Card Protection informed Bernard Zavishlock, of Abergavenny, that the insurance was only available to customers in England, Scotland, Northern Ireland and Eire, and that Wales was 'an unknown country', and so he could not renew his policy. **BIZARRE**

a little over 1000. They may be small in number, but they still want their post delivered on time.

A Brazilian businessman looked around his office for a hiding place for money, and decided that the safest place for £10,000 in cash and cheques was the litter bin – no one would think of looking there. True, maybe, since the cleaner certainly didn't look, but not safe, since the cleaner disposed of it and his money was gone for ever.

A Japanese policeman in the town of Nara wandered home after an evening's drinking and climbed into a lovely hot bath when he got back to his house. But the 21-year-old had clearly had one or two drinks too many, since he had walked into someone else's house, stripped off and sat down in the tub. When his neighbour came back to his bath he was astounded to find a drunken stranger sitting in it. The policeman was arrested and charged with unlawful entry.

GAFFES

We know they meant well, but could they have been a little more sensitive? In reaction to the terrible tsunami disaster that befell south-east Asia last year there were plenty of fundraising ventures. All well and good, but one or two stood out a little, like the Australian pop

The BBC was forced to apologise for requesting an interview with Bob Marley, the Jamaican reggae legend who died 24 years ago. It would appear that some (unnamed) bright spark at BBC 3, one of their digital TV channels, sent an email to the Bob Marley Foundation saying they wanted to do a documentary about his classic hit 'No Woman No Cry', and wanting Marley to spend one or two days with them. Bob Marley died of cancer in May 1981 at the age of 36.

singer whose contribution to the fundraising was a song called 'Climb Every Mountain', and Loughborough University's 'Swim For The Tsunami' swimathon, and possibly most foot-in-mouth, Hitchin Girls' School's organisation of a giant (Mexican) wave.

And while we're on the subject ... a ship carrying 600 tons of aid to the tsunami victims in Sri Lanka turned out to have a somewhat mixed cargo. The containers were filled with items collected by the Greek Orthodox Church, and when aid workers started unpacking the boxes they were astounded at what they found. Instead of essential stuff like tents, clothing and blankets, some of the boxes contained rubber thongs, false breasts, vibrators and bondage gear. Dimitris Fourlemadis, director of the Orthodox Church's charity, wasn't that bothered. 'Even if there were two, or ten, or maybe a couple of hundred boxes with thongs and wigs in them, that's still a very small number. Hardly worth mentioning really.'

Nutty as a Fruitcake

This is rarely a short section; the world is blessed with a strong and talented team of nutters.

'This just goes to show what the seemingly innocent hobby of trainspotting can lead to if it isn't kept under control,' said a police spokesman in the Japanese city of Osaka. When police arrested Kenji Hishida last year, he confessed that his kleptomania had begun to develop about fifteen years ago, out of his long-standing interest in spotting trains. At first, he'd just stolen one railwayman's hat and jacket so he could get closer to the locomotives he admired, but then things got out of hand. When they searched Hishida's house officers discovered more than 10,000 pairs of railway workers' trousers, and entire rooms full of hats, jackets, whistles, flags and other railway uniform items, plus many thousands of rolls of railway lavatory paper. Hishida began stealing uniforms when he realised that just looking at trains through binoculars was not satisfying him any more. He needed disguises to get closer, and eventually stole a uniform for every

dustman's holiday

Dustman Tim Byrne is very enthusiastic about his job. He's always keen to get to his work each day, but this is not enough. For the past decade or so, Tim has included in his annual holiday, in such places as Mallorca and Tenerife, stints working alongside the local dustmen. Unasked, he simply joins in with the rubbish collection and satisfies his need always to be with rubbish.

occasion, bluffing his way into engine sheds and onto locomotives. But then he started to find the uniforms more fascinating than the trains, and became obsessed with railway workers' trousers. Hishida was finally caught trying to steal two pairs of trousers from a West Japan Railway facility in Akashi to add to his collection.

To say that going over Niagara Falls is dangerous is like saying the sky is blue. So when the police officers who keep an eye on the approaches to the Falls stopped a man from going over last year, they almost certainly saved his life. The nutter's makeshift vessel was built from a car inner tube and a toy inflatable dinghy, added to a car roof rack, for stability – an important design feature – and a rug, all tied together with that durable hi-tech binding known as string. His paddle was a shovel and he'd brought his dog along for company.

Oh, dear, oh dear, oh dear. In the US city of Seattle, a man was observed behaving very strangely in a bookstore. According to a police report, witnesses observed a man walk up behind several different men in the store, kneel and start to sniff their anuses. If they suspected something was happening, he would lean forward as if he had just knelt down to get a book off a low shelf. And he was also seen to go over to a seat where a man had just been sitting, and sniff the spot where his bottom had rested. When a witness confronted the man about his behaviour, he replied, 'Sometimes I forget myself and get carried away.'

Norman Hutchins had already been banned from every medical establishment in the UK, but he just couldn't control himself and keep away. In order to satisfy his uncontrollable urges to wear surgical masks, gowns, gloves and hats, Hutchins, 53, would go into hospitals claiming he needed them for charity work or stage performances. When he was denied them, he would get abusive and aggressive, and on one occasion even threatened a NHS security guard with a knife. Hutchins got a three-year sentence, so it's prison clothes for him instead of surgical clothes.

American Billy Reed, 49, battled for 19 months with the Pennsylvania State Department of Transport for the right to have his eyes closed on his driving licence photo. Reed demanded freedom of expression and his right to happiness (or nuttiness?). A court ruled against him, but he planned to carry on with his very pointless struggle.

A Japanese man pulled a knife in a convenience store in Osaka and threatened to kill himself – unless he was given a meal of the finest sushi. The 68-year-old man, who had just set fire to his flat nearby, burst into the store claiming that he couldn't eat because his state benefit payments had been stopped. Police overpowered the man after about an hour, during which time he ate some bananas and vitamin tablets, and helped himself to a few alcoholic drinks. Police remained silent on the matter of whether he was served the best sushi.

A Canadian man had to be ordered by a judge to stop making bizarre requests to women. Gerald Naud, 35, of Edmonton, was in the habit of going around asking women to kick him in the balls. Ironically, he was jailed for 'sexual assault'.

Debu Saha, 22, from near Calcutta in India, had a strange dream, he said to police who came to

In the Italian city of Milan there is a man who believes he is a cat – and guess what? He got stuck up a tree. Passers-by observed the man-kitty up a tree, mewing piteously for help. Local kids tried to tempt him down with a nice saucer of milk, but that didn't work, so the fire brigade were called out to rescue the 46-year-old (about nine in cat years?) man and take him to hospital.

arrest him. The dream was that the flooding of the local river, the Fulahar, could be prevented by the making of a human sacrifice, which was why he went next door and beheaded his neighbour as he slept.

Last year you read about a man covering himself in Vaseline for a thrill – in this edition we present David Truscott, who got a big horny kick out of covering himself in manure. Truscott, of Cornwall, wasn't entirely harmless, though, since he also got a thrill out of fire, and his antics caused a lot of damage and a lot of grief for farmer Clive Roth. Truscott, apparently the owner of some 360 pairs of women's knickers, sneaked onto Roth's property frequently over a seven-month period. He climbed into a muckspreader, covered himself in

Julie 'Jitterbug' Pearce, 23, of the US state of Minnesota, bought a load of very useful stuff from the estate of a laser-tech engineer, and built a UFO-attracting device on the roof of her house. She told reporters that her machine's triangularly patterned strobelight design, looped radio transmissions, and laser light refracted through a quartz crystal would help guide aliens down to the area.

liberal quantities of manure and 'performed a sexual act'. Truscott also set fire to a timber shed and a barn, and the Roth family became particularly disturbed when they found imprints of buttocks in a manure pile, surrounded by tissues. A police surveillance operation was set up, and Truscott was caught carrying a bag full of women's underwear and some firelighters.

And … in the US state of Tennessee police were called out to arrest 23-year-old Michael Monn for running around without any clothes on. I say that rather than 'naked', since his body was liberally daubed with semi-soft nacho cheese. Arresting officers commented that he 'smelt strongly of alcohol'.

David Mason was flying home to England from Norway, on a Braathens airline flight, when he found himself so disgusted and offended by the rude pictures in the porn magazines he had brought with him that he just had to set them on fire. He was later convicted of endangering a flight.

Joseph Rizza, 56, was charged with two counts of vandalism to neighbours' property in the US state of Massachusetts. He was damaging trees because, as he said in a clearly much-needed psychiatric evaluation, he had 'a responsibility to keep trees from producing pine cones'.

James Kilpatrick of the US state of Pennsylvania was allegedly involved in several toe-kissing incidents. Not that unusual, especially for *Another Weird Year*; but in one of the incidents, when he kissed the feet of a 12-year-old girl, he also asked if he could kiss her liver. Now that *is* weird.

Police were alerted in the Chinese capital Beijing by neighbours of a man who seemed to have more than his fair share of cockroaches in his home. When they entered the pensioner's house he told them that he had been breeding them as a hobby and keeping them as pets since his wife had died. Health officials killed around 200,000 of the insects.

In the US city of Houston, police visited the house of Ronnie Luhn, 37, following up an investigation into the theft of a newspaper vending box. Luhn lived in a one-bedroom house with his wife and three children, and yet police were astounded to find that he had 181 vending boxes inside the house, crammed floor to ceiling. He was arrested on the spot.

In the city of Anchorage, in the US state of Alaska, a man drove his car into a wall at the Division of Motor Vehicles building, then walked in to renew his driving licence. Police said the man drove his car up over the pavement, denting the building's metal siding,

Health officials in the town of Aita Media, in Romania, were called to the home of a 74-year-old man who had complained angrily that there was a strong smell of gas in his house. There was indeed a very powerful smell, but it wasn't gas – it was emanating from the dead cow in his living room. Gyenge Lajos refused, however, to believe that the rotting cow was the cause of the smell, and claimed that the animal was his food supply for the next few weeks – he just cut off a slice of cow and cooked it every time he felt hungry. Lajos claimed he had been given the cow by a friend and had started eating it after finding it dead one day. Police were called to force Lajos to give up the cow, and he was cautioned for refusing to let authorities take it.

cracking the inside of the wall and scaring workers sitting inside. Then the man got out, walked into the building, paid his $20 to renew his licence, and mentioned in passing that he was sorry but he had 'tapped' the building.

The Red Mist

Anger is one of the seven deadly sins, and possibly the most frequently used, as our stories here show ...

It's all about friendship ... Friends Reunited, the mega-successful old school chums' website brought two long-lost best mates back together after several years, but it wasn't long before the red mist descended and Brendan Walsh, 27, was frenziedly stabbing his old school friend Noel Duff. Walsh was jailed for the attack, carried out because he thought, mistakenly, that Duff had attacked his sister, whom he had started dating. But Duff said afterwards that he still wanted to be mates with Walsh, and even gave evidence on his behalf in court, even though doctors said it was a miracle that one of the stab wounds, to his heart, had not killed him.

TEMPER, TEMPER

A German man, appearing in court in the town of Zweibrücken after a property dispute, was so ticked off by the fine he was given that he stormed out of court like a grumpy teenager, and slammed the door behind him really hard. So the judge gave him an extra fine of €200. And stopped his pocket money, probably.

Bottling up your anger is never a good thing, as the following story demonstrates. Stanford Douglas Jr, of the US city of Philadelphia, was offended by a joke a fellow worker told – and waited seven long, bitter years before shooting and killing him. Douglas said that he had been thinking about killing William Berkeyheiser since 1998, when they worked together at a nursing home, and Berkeyheiser

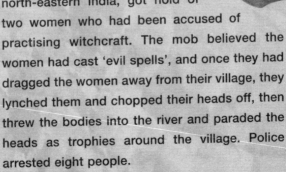

wanton violence

How wantonly violent can things get? A tribal mob in Assam, in north-eastern India, got hold of two women who had been accused of practising witchcraft. The mob believed the women had cast 'evil spells', and once they had dragged the women away from their village, they lynched them and chopped their heads off, then threw the bodies into the river and paraded the heads as trophies around the village. Police arrested eight people.

told an offensive joke. At Douglas's murder trial it was not revealed what the joke was.

There are ways and means of supporting your husband in a family dispute, even if he is in the wrong. But biting off someone's ear? Is that the way forward for good family relations? And swallowing it for good measure? In the Indian town of Hilsa, Nitu Sav's husband, Shankar, had borrowed £110 from his sister, Rekha Devi, and her husband was being very slow in repaying the cash. Rekha constantly nagged her brother for the return of the money until her sister-in-law saw red and attacked her. In the fight, Nitu Sav bit off Rekha Devi's ear and swallowed it. And we don't even know if the money was ever repaid.

Being cooped up together in a barracks can lead to close friendships, and the odd argument or two. It's inevitable. But not all arguments end up in a body part being violently gnawed off. A paratrooper in India got into a quarrel over switching off the barracks-room light: Bhupesh Rava wanted the light off after a hard day's patrol, and a colleague wanted to keep it on a bit longer. The argument culminated in Rava holding down his colleague, Durga Lama, and biting off his nose. Lama was rushed to hospital to have it reattached, while Rava was arrested.

It's amazing what riles people into violent acts – and what those violent acts turn out to be. In the US state of Idaho a 16-year-old girl was tied up and scalped with a 4-inch knife in what police said could have been an act of revenge by another woman. The girl, named only as Sheila, had a punk-style Mohican haircut, and when she offended her attacker, Marianne Dahle, she lost her right to wear the Mohican. The scalping was a genuine one – a 6-inch by 8-inch section of Sheila's scalp was cut away, and thrown into a local hot spring, where police later recovered it. Extensive surgery and skin grafts were required to help Sheila recover, but it was thought unlikely that her hair would ever grow back.

A caller alerted the police department in the small Californian town of Grass Valley that he had heard screaming, and went outside to find a woman lying in the street. He approached her carefully and asked her if she was all right, whereupon she started yelling at him then ran into her house, from which the sound of crashing and smashing emerged. So the police contacted the woman, who told them she was just having an argument with herself.

Very early on Christmas morning, the police were called to a burger van near Canterbury, Kent, after reports of a fight. A police spokesman takes up the story: 'Spiderman, Superman and Batman were involved in an altercation at 12.32 am … The injured party declined to take it any further.' The van had just run out of burgers, which caused an argument between the three hungry superheroes, recently emerged from a fancy-dress party, that escalated into a full-on fight.

AN ASSORTMENT OF RAGES

Milkshake rage

Three men were so infuriated by a bad milkshake served to them in a McDonald's in Florida that they returned there a few days later with a home-made

wife-swapping rage

Julie Rose, 37, of Yeovil, was convicted of assault when she slapped a recently arrived neighbour in the face. Why was Mrs Rose so angry with someone she barely knew? The new arrival had driven Mrs Rose to fury by refusing her suggestion that she, the new neighbour, should join in with the Roses for a bit of wife-swapping by way of getting to know the locals. Honestly, how unfriendly.

bomb. The three men, two of whom were in the US military, mixed toilet cleaner and aluminium foil in a plastic bottle and left it in the restaurant to bubble, seethe, and finally explode, spraying its contents around the restaurant, but hitting no one. Not even the person who served them the dodgy milkshake.

You're not going to believe the next one ...

Pickled kitten rage *(told you!)*

In the New Zealand town of Hamilton, a women was so enraged that police had confiscated her three snakes that she stormed into the police station to express her anger in a very weird way. You see, Susan Hoskyn's snakes were preserved in formaldehyde, and she had other jars of weirdness to get her revenge with. Hoskyn marched into the station and threw a jar of pickled kittens at the counter, smashing it and spilling its macabre contents all over the shop. Not only were there tiny feline corpses to deal with, but also highly toxic formaldehyde, which ruined two telephones and the fumes of which may have been inhaled by staff. Hoskyn was later arrested.

Parking ticket rage

The response of an Iranian man to getting a parking ticket nearly ran off the rage scale. After having made, according to eyewitnesses, frantic (and fruitless) pleas

catlitter rage

Marie Calkins from the US state of Washington set fire to her apartment, because, as she told police who questioned her on the incident, she was very angry that her cat's litter tray was full up and rather smelly.

to the traffic warden not to issue the ticket, he doused his car in petrol and applied a lighted match, instantly turning his car into an inferno.

Christmas present rage

Say it with your gun! Cameron Miller, 19, was arrested in the US state of Louisiana on Christmas Day and charged with firing shotgun blasts at his mother, stepfather and stepbrothers as they drove away. Why the gun-based rage? Because Miller was gutted that he did not receive any money for Christmas, only some music CDs.

Steven Murray, 21, of Feasterville in the US state of Pennsylvania, waited until the day after Christmas to give vent to his present rage. Furious at having not received any presents from his parents, he set their house on fire.

hairstyle rage

Also in the rage-ravaged state of Washington, Julie Anderson, 48, stormed into Stage 1 hairdressing salon, where she was a regular customer, pulled out a gun, pointed it at her stylist, then demanded $100 from the till. She took the money, fired a shot into the stylist's car, then drove to another salon and paid for a hairdo with part of the $100 taken from Stage 1 – and all because she was angry about her last hairstyle.

Luck

GOOD LUCK

A lottery conman in Romania was sentenced to three years in jail in 2001 for claiming that his winning million dollar ticket was stolen. But when Stelian Ogica was released he carried on playing the lottery and in a bizarre twist of fate hit one of Romania's biggest ever lottery jackpots. Ogica's ticket netted him approximately £22,000 – and he had written his name and address on the ticket, just to prove there was no swindle this time.

Mary Dhume got up to answer her telephone in the next room while watching TV at her home in Summerford, in the US state of Ohio. There was no one on the line, but as she put the phone down she saw the chair she had just been sitting on crushed by a pick-up truck that had missed the bend in the road where her house was and driven straight through the living room wall.

A good reason to wear rubber gloves for your chores: Angela Edwards was minding her own business, quietly doing a spot of washing up at her home in King's Lynn, Norfolk, when a bolt of lightning struck. The lightning strike was so powerful it blew a hole in her garden wall, scorched a tree and blew out the electrical sockets in the house. But Angela, at the sink in her rubber gloves and rubber-soled shoes, survived the strike completely unscathed.

A Colombian immigrant to the Big Apple, Juan Rodriguez, 49, saw the lows and highs of life on the same day. On the day he was declared bankrupt, Rodriguez, a car park attendant with just 53p in the bank, bought a lottery ticket and won £47 million. Rodriguez was in the hole to the tune of £23,500 when he won the largest ever New York state lottery jackpot.

Sandra Duffield of Gloucester was babysitting when the child in her care swallowed some unidentified object and began to choke. Apparently there was no telephone in the house, so, with the child turning a worrying shade of blue, Ms Duffield decided to drive to a phone box. In her state of panic she didn't drive with the care and attention she normally would, and crashed into the back of a van. The impact knocked the object out of the child's throat and its life was saved.

WEIRD

Forty-two-year-old Claudia Solomon had a stroke of luck when she moved in to her cottage in King's Lynn, Norfolk – she found that the immersion heater was being insulated not by some cheap lagging from a DIY store but by two mink coats worth £1000.

ODD

His wife Iris had kicked him out of their home in Queens, New York, because he could not keep track of his money. Showing forgiveness, love, devotion and greed, she has now taken him back.

A blow to the head with a beer bottle may have saved a woman's life. Sally Hampton, 64, was attacked in a bar in south-west Florida when she tried to persuade Fidel Trujillo, a farmworker, to leave the bar when it was closing time. He hit her over the head with a beer bottle, and when she was later taken to hospital for tests, doctors discovered that she had a potentially fatal brain tumour. The tumour was removed, and Hampton's assault turned out to have saved her life.

BAD LUCK

A truck driver pulled up by a beggar on the slip road of a highway in the US state of Alabama in response to the cardboard sign he was holding that read,

'Homeless. Need Help. God Bless.' The driver gave the man $1, then turned left in front of him, unaware that the truck's trailer had knocked the beggar down and then run over him, killing him.

A Portuguese student removed his car's licence plates to have them straightened – and returned to find police had blown up the vehicle because they believed it contained a bomb. Police in the southern city of Evora were called in after a local resident reported seeing a man walk quickly away from the car after removing both sets of number plates. The car park was cordoned off and police explosives experts decided to blow up the car. 'Everything indicated there was an explosive device in the car,' said a police spokesman. The car's owner, named only as Anselmo, returned four hours later while police were still cleaning up after the operation.

Same scenario, different place: Heidi Brown of Ipswich parked her new motor scooter outside the city's vehicle registration office while she went in to get her number plates. While she was inside, someone reported it to the police, fearing it was a bomb, and when attempts to identify the owner of the vehicle failed because – you've guessed it – there were no number plates, the army's bomb squad was called and Heidi's shiny new scooter was blown up. Shortly afterwards, out came Heidi with the number plates.

A Norwegian businessman flew from Oslo to Portugal to watch his football team, Rosenborg, play against Porto. In a bar, after sharing many drinks with fellow supporters, he fell into a drunken sleep and awoke to find his countrymen had sneaked his credit card out of his wallet and bought about 6000 drinks, running up a tab of around £10,000 on it.

Near the city of Bonn, German firemen found a car next to a scrapyard, and appropriated it for practice, assuming it had been dumped. They ran a training session on cutting crash victims out of their cars, using hydraulic scissors and axes to hack off the car's doors and to scythe through its roof. Then the car's owner turned up. The teenager had not even driven his car, as he had just passed his test and was in the process of renewing its MOT.

Still with unlucky motor vehicles, when a French motorist pointed his car key remote at his car to lock it and 'fired' – his car blew up! The man had some gas cylinders in the boot, one of which was leaking. When he blipped the remote, a spark ignited the gas and boom, no more car.

In the town of Baotou, Inner Mongolia, the boiler of a sauna exploded, launching itself over a six-storey building and landing smack on top of a 63-year-old man crossing the road, killing him instantly.

Romanian Florin Carcu asked his boss for the day off when Friday 13th came round in August, and stayed stubbornly indoors all day. But bad luck will find a way, and a rare species of wasp sneaked into his kitchen and stung him, causing his death.

In a macabre kind of senior-citizen-style Romeo and Juliet scenario, a 71-year-old man in Padua, northern Italy, killed himself out of grief for his wife, who was in a four-month coma after a stroke. Hours after he died, she regained consciousness.

A burglar wanted for a string of robberies in the German city of Beuel was struck down with appendicitis and admitted to hospital. He was operated on and put into a recovery ward. As bad luck would have it, the occupant of the next bed was a police officer who was part of the team investigating the robberies. The officer immediately recognised the criminal; after a swift call to his colleagues the unlucky burglar was transferred to a secure hospital to finish recovery and then stand trial.

They say that Denmark has one of the highest levels of happiness in the world. Maybe the following is one of the reasons why. A Danish IT company, LL Media, gave all its employees free subscriptions to Internet pornography sites in an attempt to reduce the amount of time spent looking at naughty stuff during work hours. Company director Levi Nielsen sees access to porn as an acceptable fringe benefit, like a mobile phone or a company car, and believes that this move will make his staff more relaxed and efficient on the job (no pun intended).

In the US state of Texas, hunter John Underwood announced that he had developed a cyberhunting apparatus. His set-up enables cyberhunters who access his website from anywhere in the world to fire a rifle at deer, antelope and wild pigs on his 330-acre ranch. Underwood said he would provide animal retrieval and shipping services, and added that his business would be especially valuable for disabled sportsmen.

It's miserable being out of work. But not for Germans in the city of Dresden, where men on the dole were offered 20 per cent discount at brothels. Silvia Rau, who runs the Villa Bijou bar, said that numbers were dropping off and that the new policy would bring back customers. And, she added, it would provide them with comfort in difficult times. People looking for discounted sex just had to show their

unemployment benefit card to qualify for the reductions. According to Rau, the initiative came from the prostitutes' union, who proposed the discount measure as a way of helping the long-term jobless out of their depression.

In the US state of California, a particularly useless piece of professional training came to light – and was halted. A local politician made a big fuss about the fact that prison guards were, as part of their job training, being set word-search puzzles. Assemblyman Rudy Bermudez quite rightly questioned how finding hidden words such as elf, snow and gingerbread prepared prison officers to handle dangerous convicts. Guards at some prisons were being told they could complete nearly one-quarter of their annual training by doing word-search and crossword puzzles on the job, to receive credits for doing the 'administrative' part of their training, but prison officials ordered an end to it once Bermudez had complained. Maybe searching for escaped convicts would be more to the point.

Victoria Pettigrew's funky new business, VIP Fibres, was started a couple of years ago, and made the news last year due to its growing success. Ms Pettigrew weaves things like scarves and blankets, socks and mittens, for people – using their own pet's hair. One client collected enough fur from his retriever to make a blanket, two pillows, a teddy bear, a scarf and a picture frame.

It seemed like nothing more than a sensible use of resources. What could be wrong in making the most of such an obvious opportunity? Morgue workers in northern India were discovered to have been in cahoots with local market traders to store fish in among the corpses in the morgue. An investigative journalist uncovered the scam when he visited the morgue, in the hospital of the city of Agartalal, asking to store fish in preparation for a wedding feast, and was given a price per kilogram per night.

A nice little piece of business was revealed going on in the markets of Hyderabad, India. The Problem Bird is a black bird that, according to the sellers, solves your problems. Buy the bird, take it home, whisper your problem in its ear, and then let the bird fly free, taking your problem away with it. Since the traders sell the birds with clipped wings, they can't fly very far, and the traders have no difficulty in collecting them up and selling them again.

Owners of a hairdressing business in Cordoba, Argentina, made a very specific (and discriminatory) request for new staff: 'Only gay hairdressers need apply', went the ad. The salon owner defended himself by saying women feel more comfortable in the hands of a gay man, and that gay staff would concentrate on their work rather than on the women.

This is touting for business in a pretty weird way: a man was arrested in South Africa for tampering with traffic lights in order to cause car crashes. The Johannesburg man was picked up after residents told police they had seen him fiddling with the lights. The man confessed to working for two tow-truck companies, and said that he was trying to generate business for them.

Complaining about unsatisfactory products is any consumer's right (in an earlier edition of *Another*

What a nerve! A far-from-squeaky-clean investment adviser from the US state of Illinois created a DVD in which he made an appeal to his clients to give their investments more time. The man, wanted for fraud, also asked his clients in the DVD not to cooperate with the authorities. He made the DVD in the sunny Caribbean, on his 62-foot yacht paid for by his clients' investments.

Weird Year we noted a man complaining to the manu-facturers of the rope that snapped when he tried to hang himself, for example). Last year a Romanian man complained to consumer protection officials when he tried but failed to poison his neighbour's dog, a confirmed and noisy midnight barker. The man, from the town of Iasi, tried to kill the sleep-depriving dog by throwing it food he had injected with strychnine. The dog did not die and the man decided to lodge an official complaint against the poison manufacturers.

Also, in the very same Romanian town, another consumer complaint emerged that was equally weird. A local man complained to the consumer

payment in kind

The city of Montes Claros in Brazil made history – we think – with this amazing auction. When a sex shop went bankrupt, the only way for the bankruptcy court to ensure that a former employee was paid was to auction off three penis-enlargers. The judge who ordered the auction, Vanda Lucia Horta Moreira, said it was the first time she had authorised such a sale, and she was interested to see how it would go.

protection office that frozen chickens did not have the sex of the bird mentioned on the label.

LAZINESS

Apparently laziness is a human right. Beryl King, a businesswoman who owns two job agencies in the town of Totton, Hampshire, was banned from using job adverts that asked for 'hardworking' people because it discriminated against the lazy. Ms King was told by a job centre that her advert for warehouse workers discriminated against people who were not industrious. She responded with understandable incredulity, and the matter was being investigated.

Corinne Maier, a senior economist at EDF, France's major electricity company, faced disciplinary action after her employers discovered that she had written and published a book showing middle managers how to survive in a large corporation without doing any work. In *Bonjour Paresse* ('Hello Laziness') Maier vents her disillusionment with corporate culture and advises her readers to choose really 'useless' jobs as consultants, advisers or experts. Tips include disguising your favourite novel as a technical manual to read in peace, or pretending to smoke to enjoy more breaks.

SHIRKING RESPONSIBILITY

The Madrid train bombings left a lot of people on the alert for repeat attacks, especially in the US, so when a motion sensor was found on train tracks near the city of Philadelphia, the FBI were swiftly called in. After an investigation, they concluded that it was put there by an employee trying to sleep on the job, and trying to avoid his supervisor catching him.

Airline passenger David Cox had, admittedly, been carrying an unusual item in his luggage – a camel costume. But he really got the hump when, while waiting for his luggage to appear, he saw a baggage handler wandering around wearing the camel head. Qantas Airways suspended the baggage handler, who had been caught on video opening Cox's bag, trying on the camel head, putting it onto his own head and wandering around the airport tarmac.

DREAM CAREERS

In their dreams, that is …

A Kenyan man in the capital, Nairobi, was finally hauled in by police after living a fantasist life as a policeman. Residents complained to authorities about the man who patrolled the crime-ridden Kibera area of

A double dose of sad inadequacy in this story: a 41-year-old Austrian man caught masquerading as a traffic cop was not only living the dream as a policeman but was trying to use his disguise to get a date with a woman. He had bought a fake cop outfit from a fancy-dress shop and made his own flashing light to put on top of his car. Add a home-made badge and he was ready to stop female drivers for speeding, by putting the light on top of his car, flagging them down and asking to see their papers. One driver asked him for his ID number, and became suspicious, and informed the police, who sent out a plain-clothes policewoman to see if he would take the bait and stop her. He did, and was caught. He told officers that he was hoping a woman who had a weakness for men in uniforms would fall in love with him.

UNUSUAL

the city at night in full police uniform. A couple of little things gave his identity away, though: one was that instead of a gun he had a shoebrush tucked into his belt; the other was that he carried out his patrols in the company of a sheep (which apparently looked a bit like a dog).

Ever heard of the Yorkshire Regional Ambulance Service? No? Well it was never a big organisation – in fact it was the fantasy brought to life of Terence Cooper, a 36-year-old emergency service obsessive. Cooper succeeded in deceiving health officials, patients and private companies by launching his baby, the Yorkshire Regional Ambulance Service, setting up an office, tricking British Telecom into installing phones, ordering uniforms for non-existent staff and persuading car dealerships to lend him vehicles for road tests. Cooper even persuaded a hospital to lend him a room, which he used for meetings with car dealership sales managers. He ran his ambulance service for two years before being challenged by a real paramedic when he had gone to the aid of an accident victim.

A 15-year-old Australian boy with an obsession for trams was arrested after he stole two trams over one weekend, drove them a total of more than 25 kilometres and picked up passengers along the way. The boy, dressed in a jacket similar to those worn by tram drivers in the city of Melbourne, stole a tram from a depot in the south of the city and drove it along a route and back, then stole another one, picking up unsuspecting passengers before police intercepted it and arrested him. The boy wants to be a tram driver when he grows up.

WEIRD SLEEP

Richard Griffiths loves to send text messages – he texts so much, he says, that it's second nature to him. But even he was astonished to learn that he had been sending messages in his sleep. Richard, from south Wales, sent a sleeptext to a friend saying he was being chased by someone, and when the friend rang back it turned out that Richard had been asleep and had texted what he was dreaming. And after watching Disney film *The Jungle Book* with some kids, his dreams caused him to sleeptext to another friend asking where Bagheera was.

According to sleep specialist Dr Peter Buchanan of Sydney, Australia, it was a rare form of sleeping disorder that was causing a married woman's extremely unusual behaviour. The woman in question, was, in her sleep, sneaking out of her house at night and propositioning random strangers for sex. The woman had no idea that she was a somnambulistic seducer, and it was when her husband awoke and discovered her in the act with a strange man in their house that it all became clear. He was well aware that she was a sleepwalker, but the condoms scattered at times around the house had confused him somewhat.

Rebekah Armstrong of London was woken at 2 am by the racket of an electric lawnmower. Then she realised that her husband Ian was not in bed. She went downstairs to find her husband, stark naked, mowing the lawn in his sleep. And he'd nearly finished it, too. Rebekah unplugged the lawnmower rather than disturbing him in his sleepwalking and went back to

Jules Lowe, of Manchester, admitted beating his father to death, but he was cleared of murder when expert evidence convinced the jury that Lowe had acted in his sleep and was unaware of what he had done. Thirty-two-year-old Lowe had been drinking heavily, and attacked his 83-year-old father, punching and kicking him and beating him with a chair. He returned to bed after making a clumsy attempt at clearing the mess up, and in the morning a neighbour spotted the father's body, which had 90 injuries to it, outside the house and called the police. Lowe was subjected to a barrage of scientific tests at Broadmoor Hospital and the conclusion was that he had been in an 'automaton' state and was totally unconscious of what he was doing.

ODD

bed. When Ian finished his bizarre household chore and returned to bed, Rebekah told him what he had been doing – he refused to believe her until she pointed out that the soles of his feet were muddy.

FATNESS

Couch potatoes, beware! When emergency services were called to the house of an enormously obese woman in the US state of Florida and tried to get her to hospital, they encountered the problems that are becoming all too typical: the stretcher was normal-sized, for example, and the 480 lb (34 st) woman was too fat to get through the doorways. But there was another, more disturbing, problem that the paramedics faced in this case. The woman had spent so long on the same sofa without moving that its covering and her skin had grafted together. So the problem of getting her out of the house for treatment for her breathing problem became considerably weightier. The couch, with attached woman, had to be transported to the hospital, and then the couch had to be surgically removed. The woman later died there, of breathing complications.

Five years after the Chief of Police in the Philippines, aware that his force were mean but far from lean, ordered all policemen to keep their waistlines to a maximum of 34 inches, he has had to go for tougher measures. Although that first attempt at getting porky policemen to slim down had a short-term effect, it wasn't long before they reverted to their old ways, and the bulges were back. So this time the Philippines National Police Chief Edgar Aglipay signed an agreement with a pharmaceutical company to supply anti-obesity drugs, to be compulsory for all obese officers for a three-month period.

Jennifer Walters, a 29 st (400 lb/185 kg) New York woman who is bedridden because she is too fat to walk, needed an MRI scan but was too enormous to fit into the normal hospital MRI machine. So with her best interests at heart, we're sure, but maybe with not the most amount of tact, her doctor referred her to New York's Bronx Zoo. The zoo has equipment for scanning elephants and hippos, he said, so they would be able to fit her in. Apparently the Bronx Zoo gets about a dozen such calls a year but it does not in fact have such facilities for its animals.

GENERAL MEDICAL MADNESS

A man in southern China has baffled doctors with his perplexing perspiration. The man, from Guangzhou, Guangdong province, went to find medical help after discovering his white T-shirts were turning green under the arms within a few minutes of him putting them on.

When two hearts beat as one ... Doctors in the Georgian capital of Tblisi discovered that Goga Diasamidze, aged one and a half at the time of writing, was born with two hearts. One is in the place you'd expect a heart to be, and the other is down near his stomach, and both are beating away normally. There is a danger, though, as there is only one aorta and it passes through both hearts, so damage to the second heart could affect the first.

Doctors were unable to find a cause for the green sweat, but think it may be caused by a parasite in his body.

From two working hearts to a living man with a heart that has stopped beating. Doctors in Russia reported last year the case of Nikolai Mikhalnichuk, who had a heart attack several years ago (when his wife announced she was leaving him). In an incredibly rare phenomenon – only two other cases have ever been reported – Mikhalnichuk's heart never started beating again, but he stayed alive. While the heart's pumping action has ceased, its vessels still propel blood around his body, and doctors at Mikhalnichuk's local hospital, who discovered the sedentary heart during a check-up, discharged him and gave him the go-ahead to carry on living a normal life.

A bizarre report came out of south-eastern Iran concerning a women who 'gave birth' to a frog. The story is that the woman had swum in water that was infested with larvae, one of which ended up inside her, although the report does not specify exactly how. The woman's periods stopped for six months and eventually a grey 'frog-like creature' emerged.

Losing 3 kg of weight is no bad thing, but even better when the weight is made up of intestinal parasites. In central Turkey doctors removed the parasites from the stomach of a young woman in what they described as a rare case in medicine. Kemal Arslan, the

A 75-year-old Vietnamese woman was taken to hospital suffering from stomach pains, and it was found that she was carrying a 50-year-old foetus. The woman had noticed a growth in her stomach 50 years earlier, but nothing came of it and eventually she forgot about it. She went on to have three children, since the foetus was from an ectopic pregnancy and thus didn't interfere with her womb, even though scans revealed that the foetus had probably lived for eight months.

surgeon who treated the 18-year-old patient in the province of Corum, said the size of the parasites varied between 5 and 20 cm and weighed a total of 3 kg. 'We had to operate on this patient because her intestines were blocked with worms,' he said.

A 63-year-old Ukrainian man was given the all-clear by doctors last year, despite the fact that he hadn't slept for more than two decades. Fyodor Nesterchuk, from the town of Kamen-Kashirsky, said the last time he managed to drop off to sleep was more than 20 years ago. Gradually he found it more and more difficult to doze off until eventually he was awake the entire night, reading the most boring things he could find – scientific periodicals – in the vain hope that they would send him to sleep. After 20 years without shutting his eyes doctors examining him said there was nothing medically wrong.

A woman in Brazil gave birth to a little giant last year. Francisca Ramos dos Santos gave birth to her fifth child, Ademilton, by Caesarean section. At birth he weighed an earth-shattering 17 lb – the weight of an average six-month-old child. Ademilton is the heaviest baby ever born in Brazil, but not the heftiest ever – weights of over 20 lb have been recorded. Ademilton's huge size was due in part to the fact his mother suffers from diabetes.

Meanwhile, the smallest baby ever thought to survive was born in Chicago, USA. Mahajabeen Shaik gave birth to twin girls 14 weeks early, Rumaisa and Hiba, with the smaller, Rumaisa, weighing just 244 g (8.6 oz) and measuring 24.8 cm (9.8 in). It was about four months before she was allowed home.

Maybe the medical profession could learn a thing or two from this no-nonsense approach: in the US state of Massachusetts, Bill DiPasquale had been in a coma for two weeks when a friend whispered in his ear a message from their boss. The message was: 'You tell him to wake up, get out of bed and get his ass back to work.' Five minutes later DiPasquale was out of his coma.

And the medical profession could also learn from Doctor Dog, aka Milo the Jack Russell terrier. Milo's owner, Mitch Bonham, 45, had an accident while serving in the Royal Navy, dropping a heavy anchor chain onto his foot. Although Bonham only suffered a broken toe, a condition called Sudeks Atrophy set in, and doctors informed him that this would mean his leg would have to be amputated. As Bonham lay at home with his blackened, lifeless leg up, his dog Milo began licking it, for hours at a time. And an amazing thing happened: one day Bonham was able to move a toe, and slowly it appeared that life was returning to the limb. Bonham's consultant was astounded when he next checked his condition, saying that Milo had indeed saved his leg from amputation, and that the constant licking had somehow stimulated the nervous system. Bonham had a few celebratory drinks, rewarded Milo with a big bone – and nurses are now being trained to practise the licking treatment at hospitals all over the country.

A doctor in Romania had to be treated for shock after he was punched by a corpse in a morgue. The doctor was leaning over the body of 16-year-old Bogdan Georgescu, who had been brought into hospital in the town of Brasov after collapsing and appearing to be dead. Georgescu was declared dead on arrival at the hospital and transferred immediately to the morgue where the doctor thought he saw a slight movement in his body and went to investigate. Georgescu was waking up and had no idea what had happened to him – as far as he was concerned, he was still having a cup of coffee with his brother – and when he saw a strange man in a white coat leaning over him, he panicked and lashed out. The doctor was allowed to take time off work after being treated for shock.

BOTCHED OPS

A German professor, on a special holiday to Costa Rica for his 50th birthday, went to see a doctor at a hospital in San Jose because his left foot was swollen. It was something he experienced regularly since he suffered from diabetes, and the condition was usually cleared up by some aspirin. However, Professor Ronald Jurisch, from Dessau, woke up in an airport departure lounge to find his leg had been amputated. His suitcases were by his side, and £200 had been taken out of his wallet and replaced with a receipt for the operation to remove his leg. Jurisch collapsed shortly afterwards with blood poisoning and had to be treated at a private clinic until he was well enough to fly back home to Germany, where several more operations were

In a court case in New York City last year, a professional dancer won damages because his career was ended by a botch-happy surgeon who made a big mistake while operating. In the pre-op meeting, the dancer and surgeon, Dr Andrew Feldman, established that the problem was in the right knee, and Dr Feldman took a marker and made a large 'X' right where the operation was needed. A mere 20 minutes later he sliced into the other, perfectly healthy, knee. **STUPID** required to make right the damage caused by the original amputation. Professor Jurisch was last heard to be taking legal action against the hospital in San Jose.

Not so much a botched op as botched treatment. A Chinese man from Hunan province named only as Chen, suffering from severe neck pains, visited an alternative medicine expert who advised Chen to eat at least six raw frogs a day. Chen lasted around three weeks, eating around 130 frogs, before collapsing with terrible stomach pains and headaches, and doctors discovered his body was heaving with parasites picked up from the frogs. He sued the alternative medic, but we don't know if his neck got better.

Briana Lane was involved in a dreadful car accident in the US state of Utah, and University of Utah hospital surgeons were obliged to remove half her skull in order to save her life. But once the emergency was over, the replacement of her skull became less of a priority, and because of drawn-out negotiations over costs and payments, Ms Lane's skull remained in a freezer while she carried on with her life wearing a special plastic protective helmet over her exposed brain. It wasn't until the state Medicaid office came up with some funds that Ms Lane's skull was finally re-attached, three whole months after the operation.

Last year a case came to light (pardon the pun) in which a patient in surgery caught fire. Police in the US city of Seattle launched an investigation to determine how a patient undergoing emergency heart surgery caught fire at a local hospital the year before. The male patient, who was not identified, went up in flames after alcohol poured on his skin was ignited by a surgical instrument. The patient died after the surgery but that was due to heart failure and not the fire, said the 'medical quality director' of the hospital.

Here we introduce the concept of self-botching! A woman came into the Chang Gung Memorial Hospital in Taipei, Taiwan, complaining of a headache. She was referred to an acupuncturist, and when he told her that one of the needles would be inserted into her left breast, she seemed a little concerned, but said nothing. The treatment went ahead, her headache was cured, and home she went. Then she returned, complaining that her left breast had shrunk from a D-cup to an A-cup – the woman had breast implants, but had been too embarrassed to inform the acupuncturist of this. And on the way home, she'd heard a hissing noise and felt damp, but had initially put that down the hot weather, when in fact it was the saline solution in her breast leaking out. After some discussion, doctors managed to use a syringe to refill the implant with saline, mixed with a sealant to prevent further leaking.

self-surgery

A Mexican woman performing a Caesarian on herself – we've seen this in the pages of *Another Weird Year*. Now this, from the same country. Pedro Lopez, 39, astounded doctors by successfully performing surgery on himself. Lopez was suffering from fluid on the lungs, which was giving him breathing difficulties. He introduced a needle in through his belly into the base of the lungs and drained out three litres of liquid. According to surgeons who checked him over when he finally got to hospital, he had performed the procedure pretty much perfectly – the main difference being that he had carried it out without anaesthesia.

QUIRKY
WEIRD
BIZARRE
ODD
UNUSUAL
strange

Science & Technology

Want to know what all those research grants are being spent on?

RESEARCH

Two British scientists came up with a mathematical equation that would lead to the perfect joke. So if you want to have your dinner guests in stitches, use $c = (m + nO) / p$. The formula was worked out by Helen Pilcher and Timandra Harkness, scientists and stand-up comedians who make up the Comedy Research Project in collaboration with the British Science Museum's Dana Centre. In the formula, c is the funniness of the joke; m is the 'comic moment', which is arrived at by multiplying the punchline's funniness rating by the length of the joke's build-up; n is the number of times the comedian falls over, multiplied by O, the 'ouch factor' – the embarrassment or physical pain involved. The total is divided by the number of puns, p. Following the equation, if a joke has a long build-up it doesn't need such a funny punchline as a shorter quip. But a successful stand-up commented sardonically that the two researchers 'must be having a laugh'.

Researchers at the National University of Singapore developed a system that allows a person to stroke a chicken over the Internet. Attached to one computer is a chicken-shaped model, equipped with touch sensors that send 'tactile information' over the Internet to a second computer near the real chicken. This computer operates tiny vibration motors in a lightweight jacket worn by the chicken. The chicken feels the user's touch in the same place as the model was stroked. 'This is the first human–poultry interaction system ever developed,' said Professor Adrian David Cheok.

Russian researchers at the Novosibirsk Institute of Medicine claimed that what may have been thought of as a perversion is in fact an excellent cure for many conditions. The scientists, led by biologist Dr Sergei Speransky, said their research points to the fact that a beating on the naked buttocks with a cane is the perfect way to cure everything from depression to alcoholism. The scientists recommend a standard treatment course of 30 sessions with 60 of the best, delivered on the buttocks by a person of average build, as the best possible way to release endorphins which in turn create a mood of happiness. Dr Speransky says he is not a sadist – it's just a treatment that works; and the patients took to it after they got used to it. The Russian team started charging for the caning sessions, getting £57 per patient for a standard treatment.

Men – they're all the same. A research team from Duke University in the US found that the male monkey will forgo his own reward – juice – in exchange for being allowed to look at pictures of female monkeys' bottoms.

Researchers at the UK's Royal Veterinary College in Hatfield reported their very useful work to *New Scientist* magazine. It's something we've always been perplexed by: they're studying why ostriches are able to run as fast as 20 mph despite being extremely heavy – often over 200 pounds – and rather clumsy in their gait. So they've been spending their days observing 15 ostriches running on treadmills. No conclusions have, as yet, been forthcoming.

A Japanese professor, Asaki Geino, last year published a thesis in which he argued that the type of pubic hair a woman has affects her personality. And that's not all; he extended the argument to claim that thanks to the shape of their pubic hair, Japanese women have been able to make a great contribution to Japan's place on the world stage. So what exactly is his scientific theory? Professor Geino groups women into five types, with the shape of pubic hair and character being linked. So a woman with pubic hair 'resembling the mouth of a river' are most unlikely to be unfaithful, for example. And most Japanese women have pubes that are an inverted triangle, which is a sign that they are good mothers, faithful wives and caring daughters. And that's what has helped make Japan a force in the world.

CLOTHING INNOVATIONS

Cellulite is thought to affect around 90 per cent of women over 30 in Britain, and the Miss Sixty clothing company came up with a potential solution last year: jeans that can reduce the cellulite from your legs. The company claimed that the addition of retinol, a derivative of vitamin A, to the fabric, could stimulate the wearer's body to produce more collagen, which in turn may reduce cellulite. The 'anti-cellulite serum' in the jeans is said to last for up to 40 washes. A leading British cosmetic surgeon dismissed the jeans as a 'cynical marketing ploy'. Surely not.

 A Bosnian man has done his bit to help reduce male sterility by marketing what he says are the world's first self-ventilating and thermo-regulating underpants. Tight pants make men's genitals too warm, which in turn lowers sperm count. But Dragan Tadic, 44, has designed the solution. His shreddies have a special bag at the front to hold the male member and testicles gently in a well-ventilated, hygienic environment that is cooler and less ... sweaty, to put it bluntly. Wear these, claims Tadic, and your sperm count will be healthily high.

This clothing innovation came a long, long time ago, is still a big seller today, but possibly the earliest example was unearthed last year. Archaeologists dug up a 1000-year-old padded bra in the Aohan region of Inner Mongolia. The gold-coloured bra was found in an ancient tomb and probably belonged to a wealthy woman from China's Liao dynasty period. The bra was made of fine silk with shoulder straps and back strings.

 In Chinese culture, last year was the Year of the Rooster. So the Hong Kong company Life Enhance introduced briefs and boxer shorts with a dragon on the front of them, designed to bring harmony to the wearer – the dragon balances the rooster, apparently. As a Life Enhance spokeswoman said, 'If you have a dragon on your underpants, you will be protected.'

We know everyone in the universe has an iPod, and now you can charge it up wherever there's some sky: a company called ScotteVest has designed a solar powered jacket with solar panels on the back that feed to a small battery built into the jacket. When the battery is full, you can then charge an iPod or pocket PC from it. You only have to stand around for about three hours in direct sunlight to get enough power – you might get sunburned and dehydrated, but it's got to be worth it.

No sting in your tail – a textile designer at Leicester's De Montfort University created underwear made from nettles. Alex King knitted pants and a camisole top from fabric made from nettles, and said the material is almost as soft as silk, and as strong as flax, and definitely doesn't sting. So no need for a dock leaf gusset then.

INVENTIONS

Mobile-phone ringtones are big business, so inventors will do anything to get a slice of the market. And in

A German company came up with a blindingly obvious invention last year: a pair of glasses that come apart to double as chopsticks. Dubbed 'sushi specs', they have detachable arms that can be used to eat Chinese or Japanese food – and if you're duff at using chopsticks you can have forks attached as an alternative. Designer of the glasses Ralph Anderl came up with the idea after noticing that eating on the go was becoming increasingly popular. The downside? Once you take the arms off to eat with, you can't wear your glasses – so you can't see to use those fiddly chopsticks! Despite this fatal flaw, the invention was said to be selling well in Japan.

Japan, a self-proclaimed 'guru' invented a ringtone that was downloaded over 10,000 times in the first week it was available to the public. Why? Because it was supposed to help women's breasts get bigger. Hideto Tomabechi, who became famous helping members of the Aum Shinrikyo doomsday cult return to normal life, claims his ringtone has 'sounds that make the brain and body move unconsciously'. One user said she listened for a week and her 34-inch bust grew to 35 inches. Tomabechi has other ringtones in the pipeline, to help people quit smoking, combat baldness and attract a mate.

A Spanish designer last year came up with a washing machine aimed at making life easier for housewives – by making men do their share of the washing chores. The 'Your Turn' washing machine will not let the same person operate it twice on the run. Pep Torres, the designer, incorporated fingerprint recognition technology to make sure the work is carried out evenly in the household and preventing the man of the house from sitting on the sofa with a beer while his wife deals with the wash. The software will only start the machine if a different finger is placed in the sensor each time; unfortunately it cannot stop the man ruining his wife's woollens in the wrong temperature wash.

Art helps us look at ourselves – and learn that we are pretty weird...

An Argentine artist, Nicola Constantino, made the news last year when she started selling sculptures made out of her own fat. Two kilograms of the fat, which was extracted from her body by liposuction, were transformed into two sculptures of the naked female body, entitled *Take a Shower with Me*.

Artists have been known to use their teeth to sculpt their artworks, but usually into materials that are fairly tooth-friendly. Not artist Emily Katrencik, though. To contribute to an exhibition in a New York City gallery, she chewed and ate sections of the drywall separating the exhibition space from the director's office, working with her teeth for 30 minutes a day, five days a week. Katrencik concentrated on thinking of the things in the wall that are good for her, like calcium and iron. (She prefers cast concrete, though, because it has a more metallic flavour.)

One of Italy's leading modern artists, Maurizio Cattelan, caused a furore last year with a work that consisted of three very lifelike plastic dummies of young boys hanging by their necks from nooses suspended from a tree in a major Milan square. One passer-by was so infuriated at the piece because of its effect on his nephew that he went home to get a saw and a ladder, and cut down two of the three children. (He fell before he could cut down the third, sustaining head injuries.)

A Scottish artist randomly vandalised almost 50 cars as part of a project, and said that the owners should be happy they were involved in his creative

Audiences at a theatre in Germany complained that the production of *Snow White* only had four dwarfs. The Altmark Stendal Theatre, west of Berlin, could only afford six actors in total for its show: Snow White, the Prince and four dwarfs. Two of the other three dwarfs were played by puppets attached to the wall, and the Prince was supposed to double up as the seventh, but only made one appearance. A theatre spokesman explained that that particular dwarf was mostly working overtime down the mine.

ODD

A Swedish sculptor created an orchestra of instruments from ice for the Piteaa Winter Festival, then had a hissy fit right at the last minute, in true artist style. Tim Linhart carved clarinets, trumpets, cellos and a guitar from ice for a show to be held in a 100-seat igloo concert hall, but when he heard the musicians playing the instruments in a pre-concert tuning-up session, he froze with anger, decided that they just weren't cool enough, got into an artistic strop and cancelled his show. **WEIRD**

process rather than angry that he had ruined the paintwork. Mark McGowan, 37, ran an exhibition of pictures of himself scratching the paintwork of vehicles in Glasgow and London. He said he had keyed 17 cars in Glasgow's smart West End and 30 vehicles in Camberwell, south London, adding that 'keying' is a worldwide problem, and that his art would draw attention to it. And McGowan had the perfect argument to accusations of vandalism. 'If I didn't [key the cars] someone else would have.'

Travel & Transport Tales

PUBIC BEETLE

In spring last year the police of Los Angeles realised they were getting a lot of car crashes caused by drivers being strongly distracted while driving, and that the cause was always the same – the VW Beetle of a hairdresser called Nelly Node. It appears that Nelly, also studying a college course in art, had taken a photograph of her genitals and had the image enlarged and put on the bonnet of her chunky little VW, whose shape the picture fitted perfectly and rather realistically. Sadly for her and the men of LA, the police ruled that her car was creating a dangerous situation on the roads and she had to have her bonnet-based ladygarden painted over.

Zimbabwe's information minister has proposed a rather original means of attracting wealthy tourists to this poverty-stricken country. Just as eco-tourism is a growing industry in some developing nations, so Zimbabwe hopes, according to a government announcement, to initiate obesity tourism. Lardy Westerners, especially Americans, will be encouraged to spend time in Zimbabwe working on farms to lose weight, then enjoying a luxurious cruise on the Zambezi river, during which they can show off their new slimline bodies. Nice idea – but will they spend their dollars on diet books, abdomenisers and slimming pills instead? Time will tell.

Some more bizarre tourist interest was going on, this time just off the Australian coast near Adelaide. Some entrepreneurial genius was ferrying tourists out to sea, where the carcass of a dead whale was floating in the waves. The attraction was to stand on the whale's body and watch great white sharks gnawing away at the carcass. Some tourists were even posing for pictures in which they stroked the sharks, intent on their feeding, on the head. The local environmental minister said he would immediately seek legislation 'to protect people too stupid to protect themselves'.

A Dutch man was stranded for an unexpectedly long time in an airport when he couldn't get onto his flight. Sheridan Gregorio had to spend five whole months in Fortaleza airport, in Brazil, after he turned up for his flight home from his holiday without any money to pay the airport tax. Since he couldn't pay the tax, he wasn't allowed on his flight; and since his ticket was non-refundable, he lost the use of that too. Gregorio stayed at the airport, cleaning restaurants by day for food and money, and sleeping there at night, week after week, month after month, until he had saved up enough to pay that annoying airport tax. And then in a fit of kindness the airline allowed him to use that old return ticket to fly home – a little later than planned.

Women commuters in Russia won a great victory against their stinky male counterparts on the Minsk–Moscow line. After ceaseless complaints that

News came to light last year of a commuter train – laughably called the Srantah Express – which has been running late every day for the last 16 years. And not just a few minutes late, either: the Chapra-Allahabad train runs five to six hours late every day because commuters simply pull on the communication cord to stop it when it passes close to their home. Commuters were hoping the election of a local man as railway minister would improve things.

they had to sit next to unbearably smelly men, women commuters were given their own train compartments, which will presumably smell of little other than roses and lavender. Stinky feet and breath reeking of onions and vodka were the main accusations levelled at the unhygienic, boozy Russian travellers.

A Suffolk man created a bizarre means of transport – a jet-powered shopping trolley. Andy Tyler, 35, adapted the trolley, which he pulled out of a river, with an engine platform built from a stainless steel restaurant worktop, to create what is probably the world's fastest shopping trolley. Tyler can travel at more than 50 mph in the trolley, also equipped with an accelerator, brake and steering mechanism, but the jet engine is so

A tourist in southern Thailand hired a car but then couldn't get it to start. When he opened the bonnet he saw the cause of the problem – a five-metre-long python entwined round the engine. Authorities spent over an hour slowly and carefully unwrapping the snake before releasing it, unharmed but a little oily, into the nearby forest, while the tourist started up the engine and drove off.

noisy that it hurts his ears. The engine is powered by gas and liquid fuel and would cost £300 to run for an hour. At the time of writing Tyler was working on a bigger engine to drive the trolley even faster.

A very strange notice came to our attention last year. It was at the car park of the train station in Guildford, and it read, 'We regret to announce that this car park will be free until further notice. We apologise for any inconvenience this may cause, but it is due to circumstances beyond our control.' You can just see the commuters cursing their luck, can't you.

An American family living in the suburbs of New Orleans owned a nice, steady Toyota Camry that they bought second-hand in 1997 and that had been pretty trouble-free up until last year, when it developed a tendency to lose speed. The car's owners, who remain unnamed, took it to a garage where mechanics found two bricks of cocaine wrapped round the car's fuel line. The bricks, worth $40,000, had started to come out of their wrapping, pressing on the fuel line. Police withheld the car owners' names in case someone came looking for them!

Young Simon Gale, 18, from Bedfordshire passed his driving test first time. Well done, Simon, especially since he had just ten driving lessons, and they were all in his father's hearse. So he'll be great at driving very slowly in a long line of cars.

For a South Korean man wanting to pass his driving test persistence paid off – eventually. Seo Sang Moon passed the theory paper for his driving test on the – wait for it – 272nd attempt. The 70-year-old took so many attempts because he is illiterate, and wasn't able to read the theory manual. So he used each attempt as a way of learning one aspect of the test, taking 272 goes over a five-year period and spending around $1000 in the process. Let's hope he has swifter success with the practical test.

traffic jam

A German truck driver was attacked by a wasp while cruising along the A1 motorway near Greven. His contortions in trying to fend off the wasp led to him crashing and spilling the truck's load – 15 tonnes of strawberry jam – over the motorway. There was a very big traffic jam, and hundreds more wasps came to feast on the spillage. It was probably all planned by the wasps.

Pranks & Hoaxes

A 25-year-old Austrian man was finally caught after a series of mountainside incidents. For months, elderly hikers in the area of the villages of Rust and Oggau had complained of a gorilla leaping out of the bushes and scaring them. When he was caught, the prankster, a local man wearing a gorilla suit, said that the area was so boring he just wanted to give people a lively topic of conversation. The man was released on bail, on condition that he handed over the gorilla suit.

Alek Komarnitsky finally came clean about a prank that had sucked in thousands of people, including a TV station. Komarnitsky, of the US state of Colorado, had told reporters around the world that he had a website that enabled anyone to turn his impressive outdoor Christmas lights on and off. Several newspapers featured his website, but Komarnitsky revealed that what users of the site saw was not his Christmas lights blinking on and off at their command, but prepared images of the lights taken from three different angles. And on one occasion, as a TV helicopter filmed from above, his wife was indoors switching the lights on and off. Everyone thought they were controlling the lights via the Internet, but it was all a hoax.

Red faces in Lithuania as it was discovered that the country's TV Eurovision committee had been fooled by a spoof song entry. Two musicians submitted the song 'Ben' – one of Michael Jackson's biggest hits – renamed as 'You', and it was selected for a place in the semi-final of the national song competition to choose a song for Eurovision. 'We don't know all the songs by Michael Jackson,' said a member of the committee in their defence when they were informed of the hoax.

An Indian teenager, 17-year-old Saurabh Singh, deceived governments, the media and the president into believing he topped the world in a NASA science exam. Singh achieved national hero status after announcing he had won NASA's International Scientist Discovery examination, which he said he sat at Oxford University. His rewards were not just acclaim, though: the government of his home state, Uttar Pradesh, granted him a 500,000-rupee award, and more than 100 members of the state's upper house each donated a day's salary to him. But when an Indian

A site of ancient Inca ruins in Peru attracted millions of tourists each year to the village of Chucuito. The splendid ruins were said to be a place of great significance, a special place where Inca women would go to cure themselves of infertility. But last year experts discovered that the 'ruins' were built just 12 years ago by the villagers to attract tourist trade to the region.

news agency contacted NASA to go over the story, they denied knowledge of any such exam, and under the weight of further investigation Singh's story began to show cracks. Singh said he flew to London on Indian Airlines (which does not fly there) and travelled by taxi to Oxford University and back every day for the exam over a four-day period. Singh told one news agency he stayed in a hotel, but told a Hindi language newspaper he stayed at Buckingham Palace. And a copy of the

A couple in Germany, stranded when their car broke down, were so relieved when another motorist stopped to help them and give them the tow they so badly needed. But the man who seemed to be a Good Samaritan was the Bad Samaritan; the Samaritan from Hell, even. He helped hook their car up to his, then sped off before they could get in, leaving them even more stranded. Worse, the mystery man drove straight towards a nearby petrol station at full speed, swerving his own car at the last minute so that the couple's car swung into an air pump, smashing the pump and badly damaging the car. He then swiftly unhooked the couple's battered vehicle from his own and screamed off into the night, leaving behind a trail of destruction and misery. Nice guy. **STRANGE** certificate allegedly issued by NASA was obtained by a news agency; it read: 'You are the member [*sic*] of NASA' and was signed by Singh and 'Chief of NASA, Cin K. Kif' (NASA's former administrator was Sean O'Keefe). So what do you think? Can we believe him?

Unbelievably (or maybe not, when you think about what this book is about) we have another story about a towing nightmare, and it also comes from Germany. A Polish tourist whose car broke down on the busy A9 motorway in Thuringia was surprised and relieved when a motorist stopped and offered to help by towing him and his car to the nearest service station. But as soon as he set off, the motorist accelerated up to about 100 mph and drove like a demon, careering across the lanes of the motorway, overtaking all and sundry and eventually crashing into a construction site. Both cars were badly damaged, but neither driver was injured, and the police were able to charge the hellish helper with dangerous driving and endangering lives.

Superstitious Nonsense

In Johannesburg, John Smit, 18, caused a stir at his school when he refused to sit part of his final English exam, a reading comprehension based on a passage from a Harry Potter book. Smit refused to take the test, worth 30 per cent of his mark in the exam, because the children's books promote witchcraft – and that's wrong.

Mamadou Obotimbe Diabikile's attempt to rob the Mali Development Bank in Bamako, Mali, was desperately unsuccessful, ending in him being shot by police then arrested. Diabikile's failure was unexpected as far as he was concerned, since he was wearing a load of magic charms round his neck that were supposed to make him invisible. The fact that they weighed around 7 lb just slowed him down and made him easier to catch.

Feng shui: a real physical fact, or a superstitious rationalisation of how we'd like the world to be? Well, in China's Guangxi Zhuang region five people were asphyxiated while conducting a feng shui ceremony in a dangerous lead mine, led by an expert there to advise on improving harmonic energy flow.

 The Nigerian city of Lagos was overrun by a rumour, last July, that spread right across the

Police in India arrested a so-called 'holy man' who had offered to exorcise demons from a woman whose parents brought her to him hoping for help. Senthil Kumar promised to treat the woman, 30-year-old Selvi Dhanalakshmi, at his hermitage at Velliraveli, near Erode, but his treatment was unorthodox even for a weirdo hermit. Kumar locked himself up with the woman in a room before stripping her clothes off and lighting camphor on her palms and breasts. Then he started breaking coconuts over her head. What with the burning camphor and the crashing of coconuts on her skull, she started to scream at the top of her voice. Her parents, helped by some local people, forced the door open and found her naked and bleeding from the head. It appears that while the police were being summoned the locals gave the 'holy man' a good kicking.

country and caused many people to get rid of their mobile phones. The rumour was this: anyone answering their mobile from certain 'killer numbers' would drop dead right there on the spot. Despite reassurances from communications companies that no such thing would or could happen, the rumour spread from Lagos across the rest of Nigeria, aided by such incidents as the caller to a radio station insisting that his neighbour had taken a call from a death number and had died the next day. Business centres in Lagos closed up 'to be on the safe side' and the media even went so far as to list two numbers that had caused deaths. The numbers were … no, we won't print them here just in case.

THE UNEXPLAINED

A Brazilian clairvoyant wrote down in a letter, lodged with a notary on 26 December 2001, that Saddam Hussein would be found in Ad Dawr near Tikrit, hiding in a hole covered in rubble to disguise the entrance. He also sent the information to US president George W. Bush. And since this is exactly where Saddam was unearthed in December 2003, the clairvoyant also claimed the £25 million reward for his capture.

A rather chilling story emerged from Scotland last year, with implications for dogs and dog-owners alike. A bridge in the town of Dumbarton seems to have become a suicide spot for dogs. At least five dogs jumped to their deaths from a high bridge over a stream in a six-month period, and animal experts admitted they had no explanation. Dogs are well able, according to experts, to judge the heights and depths they can safely jump, so for these dogs to have leapt into a 40-foot void is bizarre indeed, and in each case from exactly the same spot. Similarly, the idea that a dog would commit suicide is also not easy to accept, despite the fact that Dumbarton is supposed to be one of the most depressing places to live in Britain. Experts state that there must be a rational explanation for the self-inflicted canine deaths at this bridge, but it is still to be discovered.

Poor old Herminio da Silva, of Belo Horizonte, Brazil, got a fright when he went to his workshop one morning. Da Silva, a car mechanic, had an old car in his workshop for repairs that had originally come from a funeral company. When he entered the workshop it was clear that the car had moved over a foot – about 15 inches in fact. The car had no wheels and no battery, no one but da Silva had a key for the car, the workshop was locked and the car was on a totally flat surface, there were other cars there but only that one had moved: all this added up to a terrifying and spooky experience for Mr da Silva, who was convinced that some 'energy from the dead' had moved the car. Even the police were mystified, after a swift investigation, and brought in an expert who could find no physical reason for the car's movement.

Fourteen years ago, the body of a perfectly preserved Stone Age man was discovered in a glacier in the Alps on the border between Italy and Austria. Given the name of Ötzi, or the Ice Man, he had lain undisturbed for 5300 years, dressed in his fur garments and leather shoes and with his bow and arrow. And in the 14 years that have elapsed since his discovery five of the people who have had close contact with Ötzi have died, the most recent death occurring last year. Is there a curse of the Ice Man? The last person to die was Konrad Spindler, head of the Ice Man investigation team at Innsbruck University, who had joked that the next victim of the curse could be him. He died at the age of 66 from complications linked with multiple sclerosis. The other victims of the frozen mummy include the forensic expert Dr Rainer Henn, who placed the cadaver in a body bag with his bare hands, and who died in a road accident on his way to a conference to discuss his famous subject. Kurt Fritz, who organised the transportation by helicopter of the mummified remains, was killed by a snowslide in an accident in the mountains, in an area he knew well. He was the only one of a party of climbers to die. Then journalist Rainer Hoelz, who filmed the recovery of the

Ice Man, died of a brain tumour. The fourth death was that of Helmut Simon, the German tourist who spotted the Ice Man in 1991 while on a walking trip with his wife. He failed to return from a mountain hike and was found dead eight days later, the victim of a 300 ft fall. Local newspapers recorded that his body was found frozen under a sheet of snow and ice – just like Ötzi's. A possible sixth victim has also been named, that of Dieter Warnecke, the man who helped find the missing 69-year-old and who died of a heart attack after attending his funeral.

A Devon woman had lost a beautiful gold and diamond ring, a precious gift from her father, and months of searching her house had been to no avail. Anita Pancherz was very shortly due to have a baby, and the combined stress was too much to bear, so she consulted a psychic, Carol Everett. Ms Everett said she saw the ring near floorboards that she felt were linked with the colour pink – which corresponded exactly to the room that had just been prepared for the new baby's arrival. Although the room had had new carpet laid, Pancherz had it ripped up and the floorboards lifted – and there was the ring.

Another psychic story from last year deals with grimmer subject matter. A 16-year-old German girl was raped and beaten to death in 2003, and after a year of police investigations into 6500 men no leads were found to catch the rapist. The girl's mother took advice from a medium who claimed to have been in contact with her daughter's spirit, and was told that the attacker was a Croatian man in his mid-twenties who worked at a garage in Mannheim, close to the girl's home town. The girl's mother demanded that the police follow up the tip, and to their amazement they not only found a man who tallied to the description, Mario Glavic, but he broke down immediately and confessed to the crime.

WEIRD DUMPING

The things people throw away in a moment of care-lessness. An Australian man found more than 20 kangaroo legs strewn across the front lawn of his home in Queensland. The kangaroo legs had been skinned, and by a professional at that, judging by the cut marks on the legs, but the police were unable to find a motive for the incident because of its 'rare nature'.

Canadian police calmed fears that a satanic cult were dumping the leftovers from their rituals outside a school. Severed goat heads were twice found on a bench outside a school near the city of Vancouver, to the horror of the community who leapt to the conclusion that satanists were killing animals for their worship. But police investigations revealed that a local slaughter-house worker had taken the goat heads from work in order to have them mounted and displayed at home, but changed his mind and left them on the school bench hoping that the school janitor would dispose of them.

And in considerably more wholesome discovery of unusual dumped items, a man out walking in a forest near the French city of Strasbourg found 20 tonnes of delicatessen meats wrapped in plastic and still edible. The salami and cured hams may have been dumped by thieves who stole the lorry that was carrying them, and who were not interested in the contents. The meat was checked by health officials before being offered to local charities.

Pensioners in sheltered housing in Sussex complained that they were being targeted by a weird dumper with a penchant for gore and gruesomeness. The grounds of Ellis Gordon Court, in the town of Newhaven, were regularly strewn with animal flesh in various states of decomposition, scaring many of the elderly residents sick. Lungs, intestines, livers and slabs of flesh all appeared on the lawn, with an attendant stench and clouds of feasting flies. A police suggestion that foxes were stealing the flesh and entrails and storing it there was met with contempt by residents, who pointed out that the putrid piles usually arrived at the weekend – and foxes tend not to work in the week with only weekends free.

Oh, the nuttiness of rural English life. Jason and Claire Foster, owners of a farmhouse in a remote area of Lincolnshire, have had shoes dumped outside their house on a regular basis. The couple have no idea who has been doing it, or why, but there has been a mix of cheap shoes still with their '£1.99' label on alongside expensive designer shoes. The shoes have often been left on a Sunday, with up to four pairs left at a time, sometimes including odd shoes and even pairs of rollerblades. Video footage revealed an elderly couple driving by and dropping off the shoes, but their identity remains a mystery.

LIFE'S LITTLE IRONIES

We'll start this section with a massive irony, then get on with the little ones.

If true, rather sad: Palestinian Authority legislators disclosed that some local businessmen, aided by Palestinian officials, had been making huge profits by selling low-priced cement, provided at a special low

Linda Atkin wanted to protest about the closure of her local post office, in Brightside, near Sheffield, so she put together a petition with 1000 signatures on it and mailed it to Post Office HQ, just three miles away. When she phoned to see if the petition had arrived inside the deadline it turned out that it had got lost in the post. Royal Mail sent her a book of 12 first-class stamps as compensation.

price by Egypt in order to support their Muslim allies, to the Israelis at huge mark-ups. And the businessmen were well aware that the cement was going to be used in the highly controversial 'security wall' Israel has been building in the West Bank to keep Palestinians out.

A Romanian man, who had been on a vegetarian diet for 12 years in an effort to lower his cholesterol levels, was told by his doctor that he could start eating meat again. Costica Ionete got a little bit overexcited at the prospect of becoming a carnivore again, prepared himself a huge steak, bolted it down and choked to death on it.

Marianne Sellar, an actress employed to play the part of a vampire in a horror tour of Edinburgh Dungeons, was about to take a (pretend) bite out of the neck of an actor planted in the audience, when she saw

The city council of the town of Sweetwater, in the US state of Florida, decided to raise money by selling off all the guns that had been confiscated by its police force. But the dealer chosen was Lou's Gun Shop in the nearby town of Hialeah, identified by authorities as the nation's leading retail source of the guns eventually used in crimes.

UNUSUAL

A week after returning from a honeymoon cruise Catherine Osliffe of Lancashire had a row with her husband; he threw the contents of a vase at her, but that was nothing compared to her retaliation. She went and fetched a kitchen knife and stabbed him to death. Her profession? Mrs Osliffe was a lecturer in Anger Management at a local prison.

BIZARRE

that a member of the audience had a nosebleed and promptly fainted at the sight of the blood, of which she has a lifelong phobia.

Here's a medical condition that many men would pay good money for, but which was somewhat inappropriate for Austria's former women's minister. Herbert Haupt admitted he has a hearing difficulty that means he can't hear women's voices. Haupt was women's minister for three years and is still an MP; he revealed his weakness during a parliamentary debate, when he complained he could not understand a female colleague, and the parliamentary president Andreas Kohl was forced to ask the woman to repeat her statement with a deeper voice. The hearing difficulty means he cannot hear sounds over 3500 Hz, the range in which many female voices lie.

Patrick and Megan Hastelow from Cheltenham were both given a short-term lifespan after being diagnosed with heart disease and cancer respectively. So they went on an 18-month spending spree, cashing in their £40,000 life savings to cram as much into their final weeks of life as possible. They listed 50 'must do before you die' items and went for it, partying in Rio, renewing their wedding vows on a QE2 cruise, going on safari in Africa and so on. Then they found out that they were in the clear, Megan's cancer having gone into remission and Patrick undergoing a tricky but successful heart bypass operation. So they're alive and happy, but not quite so well off as before.

In the US state of Nebraska, a 45-year-old TV cameraman was struck and killed by a car at a dangerous junction while he was working on a story about how dangerous the junction is.

Deliveryman Steve Coles of Ealing was given a safe driving award by his bosses – a £100 gift voucher – in honour of his 12-year crash-free record. Two hours later, Coles crashed his van.

In the capital of Tajikistan, Dushanbe, a massive monument entitled 'Eternal Life' collapsed just before it was due to be unveiled, almost killing five workmen.

WHAT'S IN A NAME?

Please pardon me for quoting the name in this story, which concerns a small, sleepy Austrian village whose residents voted last year to keep its centuries-old name despite the fact that road signs are regularly stolen by English speakers who cannot quite believe what they see. The village of Fucking lies in Upper Austria, and has carried its name with pride since 1070 – so why indeed should they change it?

A Bedford couple, Mr and Mrs Peacock, realised what a massive clanger they'd dropped when Russell, the father, was searching on the Internet for famous namesakes. They had called their little boy Drew, and when Russell typed this name into the search engine it came back with 'Did you mean Droopy Cock?' Although concerned about the tiny possibility that their son will be mercilessly teased and tormented for the rest of his life, Mr and Mrs Cock, sorry, Peacock, had no plans to change their son's name.

In September, in Canterbury in Kent, Sarah Lilley married Michael Rose; in charge of the ceremony was the Rev. Hugh Flowers and the best man was Rob Plant. Blooming marvellous!

And in Hampshire, Gemma Bird married Graham Robins (a vet, but not, as far as we know, a bird specialist). Best man was William Finch, and one of the bridesmaids was Stella Rook. We would like to think the reception was held in the Four Feathers.

A man in Albuquerque, in the US state of New Mexico, won a 12-month legal battle to change his name to Variable. What from? Snaphappy Fishsuit Mokiligon, that's what. The New Mexico Court of Appeals overruled an earlier decision by a court to refuse Snaphappy permission to change his name, on the grounds that his rights were being violated.

A Munich bus driver, originally from Serbia, had his post office account frozen because his name was

A Romanian man, Constantin Putica, finally gave up his quest to change his surname because of endless bureaucratic hold-ups. You will understand why he tried to change his name when you realise that in Romania putica means 'little penis'. Mr Putica said he has now got used to people laughing when he tells them his name.

Slobodan Milosevic. He was given a week to prove he was not the Serbian ex-dictator and war criminal.

In the US state of West Virginia Kenneth Watkins was charged with killing his family's dog with two pickaxes because the dog's name, Felony, reminded him he had recently been charged with a felony. Watkins was out on bail after being charged with a felony count of grand larceny in connection with the theft of a pick-up truck. So he was then charged with another felony, this time of animal cruelty, for killing Felony, an 11-year-old black and white border collie.

HIDDEN-AWAY PEOPLE

Pop star George Michael discovered a fan was paying closer attention to him than he felt comfortable with. She had discovered a way of crawling from the outside of his Hampstead house underneath the floorboards of his living room, where she camped unnoticed for four whole days before he heard her call out his name. Mr Michael immediately called the police and had her removed.

Martha Freeman, of the US state of Tennessee, had a lover, Rafael DeJesus Rocha-Perez. Nothing too unusual about that. The weird bit was that he lived in her house, without her husband being aware, by hiding away in a wardrobe. One day, though, Freeman's husband, Jeffrey, heard snoring coming from the wardrobe and found him there. This is when things got nasty. Rocha-Perez turned from hidden-away lover into a brutal murderer. Jeffrey Freeman told his wife to make Rocha-Perez leave, while he went out for a walk. When he returned, Rocha-Perez was still there; he threatened Freeman with a gun then beat him to death.

They sought him here, they sought him there ... and guess where they found him? Alfred Blane was on the run from police in Florida, on more than a few criminal charges, and a tip-off led to officers going to a mobile home in the neighbouring state of Georgia. A woman there told them Blane was hiding under a mattress, but when the mattress was flipped up, no Blane. Officers then combed the home, with the help of a police dog, and searched every room. No luck. The freezer and the washing machine. Nothing. When officers noticed that their dog kept sniffing at an old television, they unscrewed the back to find the 6-foot Blane tightly curled up inside.

HOME SWEET HOME

Weird housing situations ...

Richard Dorsay succeeded where so many others had failed – he found somewhere cheap to live in

America's Los Alamos National Laboratory, in New Mexico, is a pretty high-security place. After all, a lot of nuclear research goes on there. So it must have come as a shock when officials discovered that Roy Moore, 56, had been living in a cave in the grounds of the establishment for several years without anyone spotting him. Moore had set up solar panels, a wood-burning stove, a glass door, a bed and a satellite radio.

one of Chicago's most upmarket and exclusive areas, Lake Shore Drive. He didn't do it quite by the book, though, since he took up residence in the beams and girde[...] spans the Chicago River. Dors[...] fter being informed upon to th[...] quaintance. When police offic[...] an incredibly elaborate dwe[...] eams that he had brought in o[...] time. Dorsay had tapped into[...] o run a TV, microwave, hea[...] game system. Whenever the bridge was raised to let a ship pass underneath, he had to hang on tight, but apart from that he lived a comfortable existence for about four years before being discovered.

A house in the US state of Wisconsin was condemned after it had been overrun for some time by a massive colony of 450 cats. But neighbours in this desirable corner of the town of St Croix Falls were not aware of the overpoweringly revolting stench flowing from the house. Hard to believe, but they said the hideous odour from the nearby fish hatchery and the unbearable stink from the neighbourhood sewage treatment plant made the smell of the output of 450 cats barely noticeable.

TWINS

Are twins doubly fascinating?

Identical twins are never totally indistinguishable – family and close friends can always tell them apart, no matter how similar they look to the rest of the world. Well, not in the case of twin sisters in Taiwan. The 22-year-old girls said that even their nearest and dearest couldn't tell them apart, and having different hairstyles and wearing different clothes seemed to make no difference. So they resorted to plastic surgery to help the rest of the world out. Doctors gave one of the pair a new nose and chin, and now everyone, including the sisters themselves, is happy with the outcome.

In the USA, twin sisters Ashlee Spinks and Andrea Springer, living in cities hundreds of miles apart, discovered that not only had they both got pregnant at the same time, but that they were both pregnant with twin boys, and that they were due on the same date. So they decided to have the four babies all together, meeting at a Georgia hospital for scheduled Caesarians. The chances of twin sisters being pregnant with twin boys due on the same date run at about one in a million.

And from twins having twins on the same day to a woman giving birth to each twin separately. Romanian Maricica Tescu, 33, gave birth to a boy in December 2004 and then delivered his twin brother 59 days later, in January 2005. Tescu knew she was going to have twins but had no idea that she has an extremely rare condition that means that she has two

Adam and Scott Barker, identical twin brothers from Cambridgeshire, took their driving tests and passed first time, with both brothers getting what is called a 'minor mark' (a small mistake that doesn't mean you fail the test). The inevitable twin thing was that they both made an identical mistake at exactly the same point of the test, stalling the car at the same set of traffic lights.

STRANGE

separate uteruses, so the babies developed at slightly different rates in each one. You'll have noticed that the twins were actually born in different years, which is also a bit weird.

Twins Elinor Stewart and Bruce Couper lived mirror-image lives for 70 years before dying just a few hours apart. Born in Glasgow in 1934, they worked in the same shipyard on the Clyde, and when they got married Elinor's husband was Bruce's best man at his wedding and Bruce was best man to his sister's husband. As the years went by the twins had three children each in the same order of two boys and a girl. And when Bruce was in hospital, very ill in a diabetic coma, Elinor suddenly and unexpectedly died in her sleep, and, as if he knew it was time to go, Bruce slipped away a few hours later.

Dutch twins Jiddo and Jefta Alberts have accounts at the same bank, Rabobank, which has 1.25 million members. Jefta had his bank card stolen and when he was reissued with another card and a new PIN number, he mentioned to his twin that the number was not very easy to remember. And, you've guessed it, it turned out that he had been issued with the very same PIN number as Jiddo, who had had his number for a few years. Neither twin wanted to change their number.

false alarms

David Page, 40, was digging near his home in Coltishall, Norfolk, when he unearthed something that looked suspiciously like a World War II land-mine. Instead of leaving it well alone, Page pressed the button on top of it, and realised, nanoseconds later, that this was maybe not a good idea and that he would blow himself up. So he kept the button pressed down, fearing that releasing it would trigger the explosion, and made his way gingerly to his shed, where he took the precaution of taping his thumb tightly down onto the button. By now beside himself with terror, the father of five dialled 999 on his mobile with his free hand and eventually got through to an army bomb disposal expert who confirmed that removing his thumb from the button would indeed be disastrous. Before long police, fire and ambulance were speeding to the area and roads were cordoned off. A senior policeman helped Mr Page put his arm and the mine into a barrel of sand, reasoning that if it went off he might only lose his arm, while his wife brought him a blanket and stayed steadfastly by his side in his moment of dread until the bomb disposal squad arrived, at midnight. When they removed his arm from the barrel, and unstuck the rolls of tape they were able to confirm that the device was part of the suspension system of an old Citroën.

NAKEDNESS

A cab pulled up at a petrol station in the Canadian town of Woodstock, Ontario, to get fuel. Meanwhile the cabbie's passenger jumped out of the car, stripped naked and dashed into the car wash, where he enjoyed some serious heavy-duty cleansing before being arrested. Apparently he was keen to have a good wash before he got home after an evening's drinking.

Police in the town of Berane in Montenegro had a naked mystery on their hands after receiving dozens of complaints about men taking late-night strolls in the nude – in temperatures as low as –15°C. Mystified police said the men were completely naked and emerged only at night, usually in pairs. Patrols in the area were stepped up to try and catch them, with no success at the time of writing.

A church minister in Australia called on like-minded Christians to join him in celebrating religion in the nude – and Pastor Robert Wright, 51, planned not only to hold weekly fellowship meetings at a nudist resort near Brisbane, but also to start a naked music festival at nearby Cabarita called Raw Cabarita. Raw Cabarita was billed as 'an awesome three-day party where clothes aren't necessary', and where even the security guards would be naked. Mr Wright said: 'I

am not trying to get Christians to become nudists, I am catering for Christians who are nudists. We are not into sex orgies, we are very well-adjusted people.'

A man and a woman in the city of Aberdeen were obliged to walk home naked from a park after their clothes were stolen. And their clothes weren't on their bodies because they were busy having sex. The man ran off, and the 23-year-old woman managed to find some newspaper to protect her modesty as she made her way through the city centre back to her flat. When she arrived, she found that her flatmate – thought also to be her boyfriend – had locked her out and her keys were in her stolen jacket. Although she had to wait in the nude for the police to let her into her flat, at least she didn't have to explain things to her boyfriend.

POO

Mystery missile: an Austrian family were gathered round their barbecue during a weekend picnic when suddenly it exploded as if it had been hit by a missile. Well, it had – a 6-inch-long frozen turd had plummeted from the heavens and landed squarely and with immense force on their barbie. The mother salvaged

The smell of unflushed poo closed down an airport last year. At Hobart Airport in Australia, baggage handlers began to be aware of a putrid smell, which was so pervasive that they assumed it was a gas leak, and a sizeable and dangerous one at that. Passengers and airline staff were evacuated from the terminal as the emergency services rushed to the scene, only to discover that the revolting smell was coming from a blocked toilet.

QUIRKY

the offending item, wrapped it in foil and notified the police, who simply said it must have fallen from a passing aircraft. But, as the mother pointed out, no aircraft had flown over their picnic site all day.

Smouldering poo! A 2000-ton pile of dung was finally extinguished in the US state of Nebraska, to the great relief of anyone and everyone who lived within sniffing distance of it – several miles, actually. The unfeasibly large mass of manure had been alight for almost four months; it was at a feed lot where up to 12,000 cows at a time are fattened for market, producing a fair amount of manure before they become burger meat. The pile of poo, 100 feet long and 30 feet wide, was thought to have ignited deep in its bowels, due to the heat energy given off by the decomposing dung. The smouldering mound had to be pulled apart over a long period of time before it finally died out, and the stench with it.

TATTOO TALES

The surname Holmes is, thanks to Sir Arthur Conan Doyle's detective Sherlock, remarkably and unmistakably well known. And even better known in the UK after runner Kelly (now Dame Kelly) Holmes's remarkable double triumph at the Athens Olympic Games, when she won the 800 m and 1500 m gold medals. So while the sentiment behind Emma Fitch's commemorative tattoo was laudable, the spelling wasn't. Fitch, 22, had her back adorned with a large tattoo of Kelly Holmes's image, along with a caption that read 'Kelly Homes, Athens 2004'. An elementary but permanent howler.

It's never too late to decorate ... after a long tattoo-free existence, Ralph Bonebreak, of the US state of Pennsylvania, finally made the leap into the world of the tattooed – at the ripe old age of 94. Possibly deciding that life was too short to be worrying about tattoos, or maybe because his mother couldn't tell him off (we assume she is not alive) Ralph, a retired railway worker, got a locomotive inked on his right arm and an eagle on his left. Way to go, Ralph.

This is definitely the first time we have heard of a crime like this. In the town of Norwich in the US state of New York, a man and a teenager were charged with forcibly tattooing an obscenity on the forehead of a 17-year-old boy. The police refused to elaborate on the nature of the tattoo, except to say that it was a phrase. The teenaged victim told police that he had been held down by a man and another teenager at a house in Norwich while they forcibly tattooed the rude words, using a home-made tattooing tool. Police said it was probable the victim would require plastic surgery or a laser process to remove the ink.

WHAT A COINCIDENCE

A Suffolk couple left their rented home at 31 Sandpiper Road, Ipswich, when they bought a newly built house that was known on the development plan as simply Plot 36, and had not been built when they bought it. When the development was complete, it turned out that Paul and Barbara Prewett were moving to 31 Sandpiper Road – a 3,000,000 to 1 coincidence. Paul said: 'I think it shows that the house was meant to be ours.'

A United Parcel Service driver was involved in a crash on an icy road near Keene, in the US state of New Hampshire, suffered a head injury, and was taken to the local hospital for tests. Unfortunately for the driver, the equipment used for the tests was out of

Sixty-eight-year-old Englishman Alf Newman was on holiday in Jamaica, and climbed into a typically battered old taxi for a ride. The clunky Nissan Sunny looked spookily familiar, and he eventually realised that the car he was being driven in used to be his own back in England – he had scrapped it 16 years earlier.

order – but the necessary parts were supposed to be arriving soon. While checking to see how soon the vital parts would arrive, staff realised that the injured driver had been in the act of delivering them when he crashed. Someone was sent to the spot where the accident happened to fetch the parts.

A story that came to light last year concerns an *Another Weird Year* favourite – long-lost family members. In the US city of San Francisco, Kari Maracic was invited to a dinner on 11 August, where she found herself sitting next to a total stranger, one Ben Davis. As the evening passed and they talked more and more, Kari mentioned her sadness at not being able to track down her long-lost brother, who had been given up for adoption. She added that the sadness was worse around the time of his birthday, 9 August. 'What a coincidence,' said Ben. 'My birthday is August 9th.' A few swift moments later and – you've guessed it – they worked out that they were indeed brother and sister.

A weird set of numbers for you that came to light last year: the foundation stone of the Pentagon was laid on 11 September, 60 years to the day before it was attacked in 2001 as part of the 9/11 al Qaeda attack; the Bali bomb was on 10.12.02, just one digit more than 9.11.01; and between 9/11 and the Madrid bombing, 911 days elapsed.

The town of Medford in the US state of Oregon was showing a classic Hollywood movie, and 1000 eager fans were packed into the amphitheatre, when the sprinkler system suddenly came on and could not be shut off. The film? *Singin' in the Rain*.

WEIRD

More number coincidences, from Australia (and not in any way macabre): Craig and Rachael Halliday's second son Luke was born at 22.22 hours, on the 22nd day of the 2nd month of 2004. He weighed 2.2 kg. And when father Craig placed the birth notice in the *Brisbane Courier-Mail*, the bill was $22.22.

SORRY ABOUT THE DELAY

This may be the longest delayed letter ever: a letter sent from a Lutheran church official in the town of Eisenach to officials in the nearby town of Ostheim, about the choice of a new clergyman, was posted in 1718. It was sent by mistake to another Ostheim, near Frankfurt, and ended up in the town archives there. Two local historians from the respective Ostheims were discussing archive material one day last year and the mistake was revealed. So Germany's postal service finally delivered the letter, 286 years after it was sent.

A Romanian man, Gheorghe Titianu, of the town of Suceava, asked the Romanian telephone company for a telephone – 28 years ago. Last year, they got back to him to say there was no line available, and would he please apply again later. At least they enclosed a prepaid envelope for him so his reply got back to them straight away.

Not True, Unfortunately

After all the above weird-but-true (as far as we know!) stories, here are a few weird-but-untrue ones.

This was the story that came out in the early part of 2005: a Romanian couple carried out a cyber-relationship for three months before meeting each other, and it wasn't long before Nonu and Cornelia Dragoman got married. So when their baby Lucian was born, the natural choice of middle name was, of course, Yahoo (shouldn't that be 'Yahoo!'?) – after the online company which brought them together. Welcome, Lucian Yahoo Dragoman. Well, that story was invented by a journalist for the Romanian newspaper *Libertate*, and that journalist was sacked when his employers found out.

Close, but no cigar. A story last year ran thus: 'In the US, the University of Wisconsin website has a large section advising students about plagiarism. Unfortunately it turns out that a lot of it was plagiarised from the Purdue University web page on plagiarism.'

The delicious irony would have made a great story but unfortunately it turned out that although some of the site had been plagiarised, it was not on the subject of plagiarism. Shame.

A diner at a Wendy's restaurant in California was enjoying a nice hot bowl of chilli when she found something in her mouth that felt a little different from minced beef. She spat it out and there in front of her was a human finger. Although the woman was immediately sick, a health officer later remarked that the finger had been very well cooked, and couldn't have carried anything to make the woman ill. Health officials also made sure to count the fingers of all the restaurant employees just to confirm that the finger, which appeared to be that of a woman and seemed to have been torn off by operating machinery, hadn't come from inside the restaurant (everyone had ten fingers!). And this was all a hoax: Anna Ayala, who had a history of bringing claims against large corporations, was arrested and charged with attempted grand larceny. It would appear the finger belonged to a relative, Ayala slipped it into the chilli and hoped she could sue for massive damages.